Rally-Point Backlog

Protect The Team
Protect The Vision
Ship

Rally-Point Backlog:
Protect The Team - Protect The Vision - Ship
ISBN 9780993606816 (eBook)
ISBN 9781549815911 (Paperback)

Published by Bookature
CP 47024, Levis (succ Saint-Jean), Canada, QC, G6Z2L3

For news, contact information, talks
and training events visit:
rallypointbacklog.com and crumbscale.com

You can also follow Rally-Point Backlog online:
On Twitter @rpbacklog
On Facebook facebook.com/rpbacklog

Have you found a mistake? The eVersions and future physical
copies of this book can be updated when a correction is needed.
Help us improve by emailing those mistakes to:

rallypointbacklog@gmail.com

Who is this book for?

The subjects of this book are described in the context of small to medium sized Scrum development projects, though the majority of the concepts can also be directly applied or adapted to large projects. This book mostly refers to the Product Owner, Development Team and the stakeholders but is also intended for the Agile leader, Scrum Masters and other project collaborators with an interest in the success of the project. More specifically:

- This book is for the **Product Owner** who wants to maximize his collaboration with the Development Team in order protect the vision.

- This book is for the **Development Team** who wants to interact with the PO as they support him while protecting the quality of their technology choices. It is also for the Development Team who wants a better and faster effort estimation method using points

- This book is for the **Agile leader** (which includes the Product Owner, technology lead, the Scrum Master and the Agile manager) who wants to create a sustainable culture through winning conditions, proper delegation, better collaboration, team engagement and risk management.

This book describes methods for improving predictability, team engagement, effort estimation and risk management. It focuses on the interactions between the Product Owner and the Development Team around the the Backlog. This book covers the pre-project time period and the project initial phase until the Product Backlog and an initial planning are created.

The development culture philosophy underpinning the approaches described in this book puts people first. In this book, sustainability and engagement overrides pressure and hierarchy.

When reading this book, having experienced the full life cycle of 2 or more development projects using Scrum is a plus. As the methods in this book are based on the Scrum framework, it assumes the reader fully understands the Scrum basics described in the Scrum Guide.

Enjoy!

Rally-Point Backlog

Protect The Team - Protect The Vision - Ship

by
Phillipe Cantin

Foreword by
Jean-René Rousseau

Bookature

CP 47024 Levis succ Saint-Jean, Levis QC G6Z2L3
Bookature.com
Edited in collaboration with Lynnea Taylor

Contents

1 Foreword

By *Jean-René Rousseau*
Director of Agility Excellence Center at Facilité

I met Phillipe for the first time in 2008. At that time he was the Lead Programmer (Project Chief) of a video game production team. Phillipe and his colleagues were experimenting with Scrum and Agile in general when I was hired to coach several teams in that studio. I was instantaneously taken by Phillipe's energy and leadership portrayed by his dedication to continually improve the team's ecosystem toward better performance and yet, never in detriment of the individuals. It was, already at the time, the roots of what Phillipe is presenting to you now as his modus operandi: "Protect the Team, Protect the Vision, Ship!"

I have crossed paths with many Agilists throughout my career, each with their strengths and weaknesses, but rarely did I see such a balance between the will to deliver effectively, the will to build high value products and the will to create a healthy, fun and engaging work environment. At the heart of this beautiful balance: the Rally-Point Backlog that Phillipe presents to you in this book, turns out to be, very much like him, extremely pragmatique.

Our professional paths crossed again in 2014. I was looking, at the time, to create a top ranked Agile coaching team that could have a significant impact on software building in our corner of the world (Québec, Canada). Phillipe, for his part, was looking for a way to extend his own impact and communicate his passion to a greater audience. It was a perfect match! Today, I have the chance to collaborate on a daily basis with Phillipe while working at the heart of large organizational transformations. Even now, although the transformation of organizations and people is not a walk in the park, there is not a single day where Phillipe doesn't show up for work with the same passion as when we first met and, especially, still with the same mantra: "Protect the Team, Protect the Vision, Ship!"

If, as Phillipe does, you have a passion to create dynamic and performant teams ready to deliver exceptional products against all odds (because indeed, building software is a dangerous sport), this book is for you. You will discover, throughout the pages, some tips, tricks, anecdotes and analogies (always enjoyable) which will compliment your Agile toolbox and, in particular, will give you that spark to propel your teams to the next level of performance. I am convinced that this book will inspire you as, on a daily basis, Phillipe inspires people around him.

It is a great honor for me to have the chance of writing this Foreword. Thank you Phillipe for this opportunity and, above all, thank you for continuously challenging us.

Good reading!

2 Preface

I call it "landing a jumbo jet".

For an airliner to land successfully, many steps must be performed and countless corrections are needed to compensate for the unique circumstances present at each landing. The goal is to land on time and not miss the landing strip but real success comes when we also kept the passengers happy and the crew healthy. Only after the plane is safely on the ground, can we relax.

Delivering a software project is the same and, using this analogy, the dual role of Product Backlog begins as the flight plan and later doubles as the flight instruments.

Over twenty years after the beginnings of Scrum[1], and some fifteen years after the Agile Manifesto[2], applying Agile methodologies is still a dark art for many. Maybe we can pin this confusion on the lack of consensus in the methods or the pressure of facing self-organization for the first time but many are still longing for a pragmatic introduction to this Scrum world. This little book is my contribution to help teams

---

[1] Schwaber. K., Sutherland J. (2016). Scrum Guide. [Online] Available at: http://www.scrumguides.org/scrum-guide.html [Accessed 4 Mar. 2017].

[2] Beck. K. et al. (2001). *Manifesto for Agile Software Development.* [Online] Available at: http://agilemanifesto.org/ [Accessed 12 May 2017].

jumpstart their Agility or, if already using Scrum, regain their momentum.

My Agile story, leading to this book, started in 2005. Back then, many developers doing the switch from traditional methods to Scrum were still self training as they were introducing Agility in their traditional organizations. As one of those developers, I went through the motions of interpreting and adapting Scrum to the reality of my projects. Not having a mentor to pave the way I read all I could find online but my initial guidance mostly came while reading "Agile Software Development with Scrum"[3] from Ken Schwaber and Mike Beedle.

There I was, in 2005, with a brand new team, a brand new project and (for us) a brand new method. I started by following the book's instructions and, after a few sprints, slowly adapted the recipe as needed. Thanks to the internet and the many Agile practitioners before me, I only had to look amidst what was already a forest of information to find the needed tools and good practices. I was very impressed with the immediate improvements of using Scrum but, even during this initial honeymoon period, I hit my first bump on the Scrum road. It came in the form of *Story Points*. Even though the basic concept of effort estimation using points (points estimation) was sound, the available methods had several flaws I was unable to digest. Still I wanted to use points so I began fixing those flaws one by one. Little that I knew at the time, making sense of points estimation by creating a new estimation method triggered the chain of events the impacted me so much it pushed me to write on the subject. Ignorance being bliss, as far as I was concerned at the time, my "twist" on points estimation was just another method and probably not a novel idea. Still, in the interest of sharing, after using it successfully a few times, I published[4] a rough idea of the process on my blog in 2009 and an updated version in 2010.

---

[3] Schwaber, K., Beedle, M. (2002). *Agile Software Development with Scrum*. New Jersey: Prentice Hall

[4] Cantin, P. (2010). *The neverending Story Points*. [online] Available at: http://phillipecantin.blogspot.ca/2010/10/never-ending-story-points.html [Accessed 22 Apr. 2017]

It could have stopped there but, after a few projects, I was again faced with a bump on the wider Agile road. This time, it was a major bump composed of two fundamental problems: (1) how do you protect a project idea (or vision) as it navigates the stormy waters of an Agile project; and (2) how can we create winning conditions for the Scrum Team to produce quality work at a sustainable pace? Not surprisingly, solving these problems would prove far more difficult than tackling points estimation. Progress only came through trial and error over many projects. Time and projects went by and, in 2013, I again felt the urge to share my approaches and the results they produced. I was unsure of the format and what started as a *lessons learned* short story only grew bigger and messier as I kept adding tips and tricks. Then, an event changed this pile of notes into a full-on book project in 2015 when, after 20 some years of software development, I made the jump to Agile coaching. Excited at the opportunity of experiencing other Agile projects, I was looking at what people were expecting and actually getting out of their Agile approaches. Much to my surprise, the results I was accustomed to were holding up very well in comparison to those other best practices. Maybe I was onto something here.

And so, I started a series of rewrites to formally organize my thoughts and here I was writing my very first book.

Agile, Scrum and project management are huge subjects and, to better explain how I scoped this book, I will compare the Scrum Team to an athlete. When involved in his sport, an athlete experiences two completely different dynamics: the training time and the competition time. During training, his goals are to perfect his skills and build up to a point where he is prime for competing. In contrast, competition time demands the athlete to be 100% focused on executing the present event. I view the transition between the project preparation and the project execution as the athletes transition between a training period and starting a competition. Because of this perspective, the dynamics of those two periods are also very different. In order to keep things simple, I chose to limit the scope of this first book to the preparation period and leave the rest for a future book (fingers crossed). By applying the methods in this book, the Scrum Team can follow a project vision from its pre-project form all the way to sprint 1. From this point, the team can use the resulting Product Backlog (Backlog) with the Scrum practices of their choice.

For my part, I can't help but be passionate about the dynamics in and around Agile projects, and I hope this can help many Agile teams or spark a conversation in the Agile community.

Thanks

I would like to say thanks to the following people: to my family who had to see me writing during too many evenings, weekends and vacation days; to my wife who inspired me to write and soldiered through the editing process; to my beta readers whose minds are forever contaminated with the early version of the manuscript; and to my employers and coworkers who were my laboratories and guinea pigs over the last 12 years.

3 Road to Rally-Point

An idea is a fragile thing. It must be handled with care and protected through every step before, during and after development. It needs a champion who believes in it and can sell it to others, coaxing them into following him through this great endeavor. It needs a team of artisans to bring it to life and carry it to the finish line. Everything will be in the way: politics, budget, capacity management, egos, technology, work culture, the inability to get your hands on some stupid office supply and sometimes... even you.

When was the last time you were part of a successful software development project? I admit, asking this question is bordering on pointless, considering we all have our definition of 'success'. Let's try again by asking it in a different way. When was your last project where the necessary features were delivered on time and on budget, with the client and the team both proud of the quality level and where the team was engaged while working at a sustainable pace? Here, many people will say "it is impossible to please everybody" and "perfection is an unreasonable expectation". In some ways they are right, maybe perfection is aiming a little too high. Take the game of golf for example where a successful round is not 18 holes in one. Even when measuring the success for playing a single hole, the bar of success is not the hole in one. It is then normal to have ups and downs and a good game is one where you don't fall into a slump and where the overall average is good enough to have a shot at winning. Coming back to software development, what is this "good enough" we could call success? There must be an attainable line that we all agree upon beyond which we have success. How about this one: When was your last project where the vision did not have to be maimed and slashed during production by barely holding on to the basic features? Where the dates and budget were met without resorting to extreme measures and crippling other projects? Where the quality of the solution and the code were actually good enough and employees didn't have to frame their opinion in sentences like 'This is not the best we can do but, given the circumstances...'? Finally, where it is normal for the people involved in the project to ship without putting their health and family life in danger?

Based on this, the following points should be part of a "good enough" definition success:

- Quality product
- Respect of due dates and budget
- Team engagement
- Sustainability

We will come back to the definition of success a little bit later but, for now, let's agree that delivering a successful software development project is not a simple thing. Even for teams using an Agile framework like Scrum, shipping software is not an easy task especially if the surrounding organization is not Agile itself. Maybe the key is not changing the entire context of a software project but to ensure some kind of minimal success conditions for a Scrum team to function no matter what their context is. This is one driving motivation behind this book.

We may not want to change the entire context of a project, but we also can't ignore it. As we know, understanding the environment surrounding a problem is key to solving it and in this case it is a pretty big environment. Trying to establish winning conditions for the creation of a Product Backlog (Backlog) extends the context to the whole development project including parts of the organization structures like project management, resource management, processes and stakeholders. For practical purposes, this book will take a slice of this enormous context, looking at things solely from the Agile team's perspective. From that vantage point, we can focus in further, only considering what is essential for predictability and team engagement.

3.1 Three Methods

It was not my intention to create a monster method impacting all aspects of projects. It started with a points estimation method followed by tips and tricks for creating a Backlog which lead to the need for creating winning conditions. In its current state, this approach is described by three methods focused around the Scrum Team members acting on the Backlog and dealing with the stakeholders. Those three methods aim to to maximize the team's Agility while collaborating with their context no matter if it's Agile or not. The first method, **Handle It or Hand It Over**, lists the basic winning conditions as a project progresses through each of its periods. The second method, **CrumbScale Backlog** (which started me on this whole undertaking), targets the initial creation of the Backlog and the assignment of Story points. The third and final method, **Easy-Normal-Hard**, helps manage complexity within the Backlog.

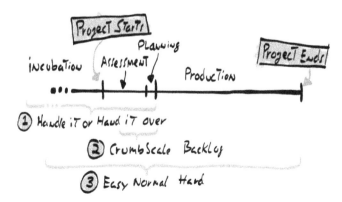

Figure 3.1 – The 3 methods in relation to the project timeline

In Figure 3.1 you can see a development project timeline where some key moments and periods are identified. We will go into the detail of this timeline later but for now we can all relate to it by recognizing that it contains a project start, a project end and some sort of preparation period (assessment and planning) before a production period. We can also see, in the same Figure 3.1, how all three methods align along the timeline and that they are overlapping each other. Because each method can be used independently or in combination, it was preferable to explain them separately and let the reader combine them however he sees fit. This, of course, may create a sense of "déjà vu" as we will revisit the same parts of the project timeline while describing each method.

In our team-centric and Backlog-centric perspective, the necessary ingredients for the three methods are boiled down to only the Backlog, the Product Owner (PO), and the Development Team (Dev Team). As for the Scrum Master, his role remains mostly the same but is now extended to cover this approach. Another important actor, the stakeholder, lies outside of the Agile project but will have a great impact on it. For the sake of simplicity, the three methods will only define the stakeholders through their critical interactions with the Scrum Team as they are the source of most requirements and constraints.

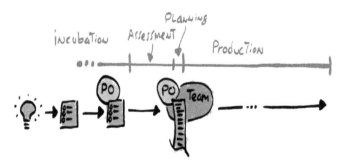

Figure 3.2 – The Backlog, the team and the PO at the core of the Agile project

10

In a generic scenario, as displayed in Figure 3.2, a vision idea will appear in the organization and eventually be described through a list of features and constraints. This list will eventually be matched with a PO in order for him or her to master the vision. As the project gets started, the Dev team will join the PO and turn the Features List into a Backlog. Reducing the core of the Agile project to only three parts was an organic process stretched over many projects. As those three parts are underpinning every aspect of the Rally-Point Backlog approach, let's explain their importance.

3.2 Product Backlog

I have seen good and bad Backlogs and I have seen projects succeed and fail. I'm not claiming that all successful projects had good Backlogs but I did find something in common with the successful ones. In good projects, people felt respected and were fully engaged. Supporting this level of collaboration and enthusiasm, I found that clarity, focus and priorities were key motivators.

What is the trick? Is there a secret recipe? There must be as many good approaches as there are good teams but time and time again, I personally experienced good results by having the PO and the Dev Team build and maintain the Backlog collaboratively. At face value, this is nothing new. The twist is all in the presentation and the metaphor needed around the Backlog and the act of creating it. It starts when I set the PO as the defender of the stakeholders interests and ask him to respect the Dev Team's expertise. Then, I set the Dev Team as the defenders of the technological quality and ask them to respect the stakeholders' needs. Together, they transform the initial features, use cases and requirements into a series of Stories and Epics.

The buildup to the metaphor is further supported with each Story using the 'As a...I want...so that...'[5] format where the 'I want...' part must describe the functionality in a business language understandable by the Dev Team and where the 'so that...' part must describe the value gained by this Story in the business language of the PO. By systematically creating the Backlog in such a way, we complete the metaphor as we now have a single document in the language of business and the language of technology. It's their Rosetta stone. Let's take a little detour to understand what this means.

Egyptian hieroglyphs were used from the 32nd century BC until the 4th century AD and, sadly, were forgotten during the 5th century. Around 12 centuries later, in 1799 to be exact, something happened which helped us understand this lost writing system. The Rosetta Stone[6] stele was found. It was a single piece of rock roughly the size of an office desk surface on which was engraved three paragraphs, each written in a different script: Greek, Demotic and ancient Egyptian hieroglyphs. What was amazing about the Rosetta Stone is that each script is a translation of the same text. One point of reference, one piece of information, three languages. Our understanding, or should I say relearning, of Egyptian hieroglyphs accelerated greatly, thanks to the study of this artifact.

---

[5] Cohn. M. *User Stories*. [Online] Available at:
https://www.mountaingoatsoftware.com/agile/user-stories [Accessed 4 Jan. 2017].
[6] Wikipedia. *Rosetta Stone*. [Online] Available at:
https://en.wikipedia.org/wiki/Rosetta_Stone [Accessed 4 Mar. 2017].

Figure 3.3 – The Rosetta Stone

When the creation of the Backlog is done through a deep collaborative effort between the PO and the Dev Team, it becomes more than a Scrum artifact. By describing the project in two languages, it turns into an agreement between technology and design describing a single vision where both sides are respected. It is their Rosetta Stone, their rallying point, engaging them to maintain it throughout the project for it to remain the single point of reference. Once this engagement is created, everything will be revolving around the Backlog. Sentences like "Let's put it in the Backlog" will mean something and the progress measured from this Backlog will speak to both the Scrum Team and the organization. In effect it becomes the rally-point for anybody involved in the project. Also, such a relevant Backlog will act as a change management tool as it helps everybody involved to understand and follow the ups and downs of the project.

Throughout my career it was always important for me to believe in the vision. It was also important to understand how my work related to this vision. Without that, work would become routine or, even worse, a burden. To achieve this goal I made sure the Backlog was a true representation of the vision. This fulfilled my need to be an active participant. It is no surprise then that, as soon as I was responsible for a team, I projected this need onto them. The team members are not just pairs of hands typing on keyboards, they are brains attached to pairs of hands typing on keyboards. Why would they only be doers when they can collaborate, challenge and contribute? This way they can add a unique value to the project and make it better while making it theirs. Having the Dev Team participate in building the Backlog is my strongest tool as an Agile leader.

3.3 Development Team

I understand through experience what it's like to be a member of the Dev Team. This is probably why, every time I can, I will engage them in the project as early as possible. How early? If all goes well, it starts with the Backlog creation in close collaboration with the PO. The result of this work will reveal a new face of the original vision, morphed with the reality of what is feasible for the Dev Team. John Lasseter, Chief Creative Officer at Pixar and Disney, described this collaboration process in a very clever way: "*The art challenges the technology. The technology inspires the art.*"[7] With a little tweak (I'm sure John won't mind), I generalized this to fit all cases of development:

'The vision challenges the technology and the technology inspires the vision.'

A good reason to engage and collaborate with the Dev Team is to promote a work culture protecting the individuals and the teams. It may sound normal for some, but you don't have to look too far to find organization cultures where profit wins over

---

[7] *The Pixar Story.* (2007). [DVD] Sonoma: Leslie Iwerks Productions

people. When people are in lower priority it often creates sharp divides between management, employees and departments. In such an environment, engaging a team is pretty difficult. Yet, if it does happen, you will probably find that this so-called 'engaged' team has probably grown with an "us versus them" mentality. In this kind of environment, ownership overrides collaboration and energy is spent on the definition of borders instead of producing value. Not surprisingly, this is not an effective or collaborative work culture.

Another gain of engaging the Dev Team into the project is the increase in alignment between business and IT which, if we consider the State Of Agile Survey[8] in the last 10 years, is one of the top 6 reasons why organizations are adopting Agile.

As an Agile leader, caring for my team and pushing to engage them sounded good but, for the longest time, I felt like an outsider amongst the other leads. My teams were happy but, compared to other leads, I was a black sheep. It took some time to pinpoint why, but I finally realized it was because I always put people first. For the last 12 years, all my decisions have been driven by this simple set of rules:

Protect the team
Protect the vision
Ship

Figure 3.4 – Standing Orders

Nowadays, I'm still a black sheep but at least I know why and I'm totally fine with it.

---

[8] VersionOne. (2017). *11th Annual State of Agile Report*. [Online] Available at: https://explore.versionone.com/state-of-agile/versionone-11th-annual-state-of-agile-report-2 [Accessed 28 May 2017].

In the army, Standing Orders[9] are not given to any particular person but apply all the time to all personnel under the General who made the order. It is a way to enforce something that is not covered by the standard rules. I use this concept to bend work culture toward respecting people, not compromising on quality and actually reaching goals. Those are my standing orders, and I make them clear to all my teams and, especially, the leaders working under me.

> *On a side note, back around 2012, I was happily swimming against the current at my workplace with my heretic priorities when I found out about project Protei (now Scoutbots). It is an open source, open hardware project with the purpose of building autonomous drone boats to clean oil spills and plastic pollution from the oceans. Other than the fact that they are building robotic boats the one thing that excited me about this organization was its ethical order of priorities:*

> *1 – Nature*
> *2 – People*
> *3 – Technology*
> *4 – Money*

My definition of an Agile leader puts people first and teams first. Always.

For those of you who have been under the pressure of shipping a project, you know how backward this order of priority is compared to what drives many project decisions. This is sad but not hopeless. Since decisions are made at many levels, you will always be able to positively affect all the people within your range of influence. On the down side, following these guidelines puts extra pressure on you as a leader, initially at least, while you create this culture around your team. You, as a

---

[9] Wikipedia. General Order. [Online] Available at:
https://en.wikipedia.org/wiki/General_order [Accessed 4 Mar. 2017].

person of influence in your organization, will have to work a bit harder to defend the team and the vision.

I'm using this set of priorities for two purposes. The first purpose is for decision making during the project. When any decision is made I'm asking myself: Will this hurt the team? Will we still have a quality vision? Can we still ship on time and on budget? The second purpose is similar to a general *Definition of Done*[10] regarding the success of a project. A project is successful if quality is shipped on time, on budget with an engaged team. Engagement, in a culture where people comes first, implies having a sustainable pace.

Quality shipped on time, on budget with an engaged team

Figure 3.4 – Definition of success for a project

---

[10] Gupta. M. (2008). *Definition of Done: A Reference*. [Online] Available at:
https://www.scrumalliance.org/community/articles/2008/september/defi nition-of-done-a-reference [Accessed 18 Jan. 2017].

17

3.4 Product Owner

As one of the only three roles in Scrum, the PO plays an important part. Yet, looking at the sea of information you can find about the Scrum Master and the Dev Team, this particular member of the Scrum Team is often misunderstood and, being overlooked this way, the intricacies of his work can often be underestimated. Personally, I have played the PO role many times and, as many of my coworkers can attest too, could go on a massive tangent on this subject. Thanks to the magic of editing, in this book I have stayed on track and only looked at the PO from the perspective of the Backlog creation and within the scope of the three methods.

Minimally, it is important to understand that the PO takes care of the Backlog which must survive and adapt to change whether it comes from within the project (within the Scrum Team) or from the stakeholders (or clients). All this change must eventually be handled at the Backlog level in order to respect both the requirements needs and the technical possibilities. The PO, like the Backlog, is at the middle of this interaction.

To have an efficient (or might I say Agile) problem solving situation, communication between the stakeholders and the Dev Team is key. The feedback loop should be as dynamic and short as possible. By applying Scrum out of the box, technical problems are covered, since the communication channels needed reside within the Dev Team. Vision problems are also covered with the communication channel created between the PO and the Dev Team. Finally, the business problems require a communication path between the Sponsor-type stakeholders and the PO in order to impact the Backlog. Those types of business problems (e.g. shifting delivery date or staffing changes) will often reach the PO (and through him the Dev Team) through a management role like the Project Chief, the team lead or even sometimes the Scrum Master.

The Backlog must incorporate the requirements and constraints of all three types of stakeholders: vision, business and technical. Even though the PO is strongly connected to the vision side of this trio, he still must compose with all three to keep the Backlog relevant. From an organization perspective, the PO's expertise is to maximize the output value of the product while other people in the organization are tasked with maximizing the output value of the organization as a whole. Through the Backlog content and maintenance, the PO is empowered for adapting to project scale problems only. This is where this book is adding to the PO's definition.

When an organizational scale problem arises, the PO can demonstrate the effects through the impacts on the Backlog. If a business decision ultimately results in a negative effect on the Backlog, the PO must translate this into concrete impacts on scope, value, due dates, budget, resources and staffing. But here is the twist. When communicating with the stakeholders, the PO does not only bring bad news but also possible solutions. The PO is the expert at understanding how far the project can bend to help the organization while still succeeding. He also can ask for both the Dev Team and the business side to help him. The Dev Team can propose alternative ways to do things while the business side can help by changing parameters like scope, due dates, budget, resources and staffing.

This is not direct communication between the Dev Team and the Sponsor-type stakeholders but it is better than the standard one-way, top-down communication we are used to seeing.

The PO was already the ambassador of design posted in Dev Team's country. Now we are asking him to maintain a bilateral dialogue with the business empire.

The PO described in this book is rooted in the Scrum Guide description of this role, but here we should clarify the importance of collaboration in the PO's job. When you read the Scrum Guide (once a year like we all should) the PO's role may look simple but, if you have lived through enough projects, you know that a single person is often not enough to fill these shoes. What to do then since the Scrum rules are clear about having a single PO? As the guide specifies, one person must be in charge of making the final decision for the Backlog but nothing is preventing him from asking for some help. For this, having a constant and clear communication with the Dev Team and the stakeholders is key to maintain a relevant prioritization. Let's look at a couple concrete examples of projects where the PO needs help to manage the Backlog.

First, imagine a technology-oriented exploration project where the PO may have a handful of user level features while the vast majority of the Backlog will be filled with technical work.
For the sake of simplicity let's call the PO stories "Business Stories" and the others Technical Stories (A.K.A. non-functional requirements or NFR). To maximize value in a technical project of that sort the PO will rely on one or many of the Dev Team experts to create the Technical Stories and link them to the Business Stories. The PO will also need the team's help to cut those 'prerequisite' Technical Stories into vertical increments[11] of value and not leave them as one monolithic sequence of events. Once this is done the team will then help the PO prioritize the Technical Stories by explaining the cost (or sometimes the impossibility) of placing them in a different order. As a PO in many successful technology-oriented exploration projects, I can say that, the full collaboration between the PO and the Dev Team is key to victory.

Another example would be the development of a product which has a business value in multiple domains of expertise. Finding a PO that deeply understands each domain is not always possible. Similar to the preceding example, the PO will need help but, this time, from experts outside the Scrum Team to assist him in maximizing the value of each subject and of the Backlog as a whole. Contrary to the previous example, you may also have the problem of choosing between more than one possible PO. In such situations the person with the knowledge that covers the majority of the Backlog would be the

---

[11]   AgileAlliance. *Incremental Development.*, [Online] Available at:
        https://www.agilealliance.org/glossary/incremental-development/
        [Accessed 4 Mar. 2017].

best choice. A good set of qualities for a PO in this kind of situation is to know where to find the necessary information, to manage outside pressure and the ability to create and defend a vision covering the project as a whole.

This situation will happen more in large work structures and it is a slippery slope towards the 'design by committee' scenario where the PO is a powerless puppet. When explaining this to my teams and clients, the actual term I use to describe this job situation is to be a Backlog b**ch. Yes... it's that bad. The organization can prevent this by empowering and supporting the PO's role.

No matter if the PO needs help or not, the resulting Backlog will need to be meaningful for both the stakeholders and the Scrum Team. For the Backlog to become and remain meaningful, something should be said about the leadership qualities needed to be a good PO. It comes down to this: a strong PO will define and sell the "adapted" vision to the Scrum Team and to the stakeholders. "Wait what? Adapted vision?". Let me explain how I see the PO's role and responsibilities. Picture a project as a symphony to be performed by a full orchestra. Also, for the sake of argument, let's imagine this music was created by a composer who didn't know which orchestra would be performing the piece or who would be directing this orchestra. In order to play the music, the director must deeply understand the author's intent and adapt the piece to his orchestra. Even if the ultimate goal of the director was to to stay as true as possible to the original vision of the composer, he still has to cope with the orchestra's strengths and weaknesses. This adaptation will sometimes happen by pushing the musicians to try new things while sometimes, small tweaks will be done to the piece itself. At one point in time this director and this orchestra will have uniquely mastered the piece. Switching either the director or the orchestra would force a new learning process producing another unique way of mastering the music piece.

In this analogy, the composer represents any stakeholders (e.g. clients, software architects, ...) defining and impacting the guiding principles of the project. The original music sheets are the project requirements which, in the context of software development, I will refer to as the project vision. The orchestra is an Agile Dev Team executing a project. Finally, the director (A.K.A. conductor) is the PO. The result of their combined efforts described by their common experience and their sheets of music covered with annotations, represents the Backlog. The Backlog now contains an "adapted" version of the vision. The PO's role in this method is essential. He will rally everybody around this adapted vision of the product ensuring everyone involved understands it, believes in it and are excited about being part of it. Without constant care from the PO, the Backlog and the project vision it holds will get blurred by the ever changing circumstances. Through Backlog maintenance and continuous communication, the PO will preserve a direct link between the two realities of the Dev Team and the stakeholders, keeping them informed with the state of the adapted vision and the logical path it is following.

As you can see, I put a lot on the PO's shoulders as I would on anybody in such a leadership position. In my book (wait a minute... I can actually say that now... cool), any project needs a vision leader and a morale leader. The PO always felt like a natural choice for the vision leadership as he is selling and defending the vision. Optionally, you can have a two for one if your PO turns out to also be a morale leader. As a final thought on the PO, even though it is a one person job, I would recommend having a second person always ready to pick up the role. Like an assistant PO. This will remove the PO as being a single point of failure.

So there we have it: a Backlog, a Dev Team and a PO. Three Rally-Point Backlog main components at the center of the project. Now let's turn our focus to the sequence of events around projects.

4 Same Context - New Point of View

"If [the generals] rule armies without knowing the arts of complete adaptivity, even if they know what there is to gain, they cannot get people to work for them." [12]

- Master Sun Tzu

As a project marches forward, a mountain of tasks and decisions are expected to be completed. If they become problematic, some of those items can harmlessly slide while others can turn into blocking issues. To avoid tackling the whole mountain, we will from our team centric vantage point, limit our scope to the tasks and decisions impacting the team and their capacity to create a good Product Backlog (Backlog). Simplifying things even more, we will focus only on the details that can make or break the project's success (see Figure 3.4 for definition of success).

If you have worked on software development, you know that the notion of a perfect project is science fiction. The following method also assumes imperfection as it lists basic deliverables for each period of the project. Using this baseline to organize and measure progress and scope will help us know if we are within the limits of the Scrum Team capabilities. This chapter will also explain how to handle the transition moments where empowerment and ownership should be passed from one project period to the next. The following Figure 4.1 is is an overview of those periods.

---

[12] Tzu. S. (2003). *The Art Of War - Translated by Thomas Cleary*. Boston, London: Shambhala, pp.132-133.

23

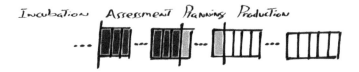

Figure 4.1 – Major Project Periods

Without going into too much detail, let's have a look at those periods. It starts with the **Incubation Period**, before the project has officially started, when the vision is unclear and not yet scheduled as a concrete project. At that point feasibility might also be a concern. Next is the **Assessment Period** when the organization has given a green light to start the project and (minimally) investigate the rough details of how the vision could be realized. During this busy time many project preparation activities are taking place. Theories may be investigated and the scope of the project should be confirmed. If all goes well, this is followed by the **Planning period**[13] enabling the team to construct an actionable Backlog of User Stories detailed enough to forecast the success of the project. Finally the project can transition into the **Production period** where the development iterations are performed. In this method, we will follow the progress of the project vision through the first three periods as it morphs from high level functionalities and constraints all the way to a pragmatic Backlog. Even though the Backlog will be in constant state of evolution throughout the Production Period, this book focuses only on the Backlog creation.

The choice to exclude the Production Period was not an easy one. However, the transition between the initial creation of the Backlog and the production iterations is a natural stopping point where the dynamics switch dramatically (i.e. preparation vs execution). If all goes well, this could be the subject for another book entirely. How about "Rallypoint Backlog - Sprint

---

[13] Note that both Assessment and Planning periods are sometimes combined into a single period

Dynamics"? Yeah I like that, but for now, let's concentrate on the creation of the Backlog.

4.1 METHOD 1: Handle It or Hand It Over

As its name suggests, this method keeps the right pressure on the right people. To do so, we will need to understand the necessary deliverables of the first three periods and the consequence of missing those deliverables.

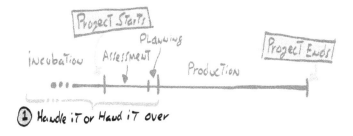

Figure 4.2 – Method 1 in relation to the project timeline

The goal of this method is to prevent pushing pressure downstream. To achieve this, we will ask from the people accountable in each period to either handle the necessary deliverables (**handle it)** before the end of the period. If impossible, we will ask them to have have a plan-b to **hand over** the ownership down the line, keeping them accountable but forcing them to empower somebody to complete the task. Here, pushing problems forward is counterbalanced by increasing the decision power downstream.

With this in mind, we will now look at the minimal deliverables needed for the creation of a Backlog as it traverses the project periods: the Incubation period, the Assessment period, the Planning period, and the Production period.

25

Because a project success is "Quality shipped on time, on budget with an engaged team", any action or decision that endangers this goal must be prevented or balanced out by another corrective action. It's like balancing a long stick on your hand. To keep it there you have to continuously do small corrections. From time to time the stick will move way out of balance and your next correction should be proportional in order to come back to a state where only small corrections are needed. In a project, an imbalance should never cross over into the following project period. Consequently, a key principle of this method is to treat the period's contents and deadline as hard deliverables with a hard date. All issues from a given period must be resolved before the end of the period. Resolution can be achieved two ways: 1) whoever is responsible for the production of this work must take care of it on time (handle it) or 2) pass it down to the next period and empower others to take care of it (hand it over). Normality is option 1 while the exception is option 2. We do not want to get comfortable with using option 2 as it pushes extra work on the wrong people and creates an unsustainable dynamic.

Respect is the key here. Imagine we are working on a two steps process. I'm taking care of the first step and you complete the production by executing step 2. Now let's assume we have defined the minimal work for step 1, before handing it down the chain to you. If this minimal work is incomplete or not done, it will impact your productivity and also prevent you from concentrating on step 2.

Before looking at the proper way to deal with such events, let's remind ourselves some classic wrong ways of handling this. If I send incomplete work to you, expect you to do 'my' work and then proceed to look over your shoulder and nitpick at how 'you' are doing it, this is not efficient. This is what I call the 'This is not how I would have done it' syndrome.

Also, if I now add a validation step to 'ensure' that your are doing 'my' work correctly, this is disrespectful. I call this one the 'I need to approve my work which you are doing' syndrome.

Then we have the classic one where my work is backing up and, late in the project, I push it all in one big batch expecting you to still deliver on time. This one is the 'I just did a big push so why don't you?' syndrome.

And so it is, as the imperfections increase, you must proportionally redistribute decision power which can even include scoping powers. This way, people on the receiving end are empowered to correct the problem within the allocated time of the original points estimation. This can prevent a bad transition from slipping even further and, in a domino effect, impact more people down the line. When describing this approach I often say "If I give you incomplete work, you will also get the free reign to resolve the impacts". This way of managing transition puts the pressure upstream on the appropriate people, forcing them to either complete the necessary work or make proportionate concessions. Entering the project, each part of the chain agreed to a certain level of personal risk while accepting a certain level of manageable unknowns. Each part of the chain is then expected to plan and handle their way around the unknowns arising in their part of the work. When hit with something too big to handle, it is important to recognize the impact spreading to other teams. If this happens to you, as long as the problem was in your hands, the best solution was very likely going to come from you or your Scrum Team. Now that the problem has spread, you must recognize that the best solutions will most likely come through collaboration with the impacted people.

Other than the importance of learning from your mistakes so they are not repeated, it does not really matter why the initial problem occurred, but it should be a rule not to simply push it down the line. *Handle it or hand it over* is about finding the root cause and not about pointing a finger.

Now we will look at the minimal work that must be handled in each project period.

4.2 Incubation Period

This is the forgotten part of a project's life. Most methods will describe the beginning of a project as the moment when the budget is allocated and a team is assigned to it. This is only the start of the active phase but what about the passive phase that preceded it? Can actions or inactions during the Incubation Period affect the Product Owner (PO), the Development Team (Dev Team) or the creation of the Backlog? Yes it can. To understand how, let's look at the bare minimum of work needed and the transition to the Assessment period.

Every idea and project starts in some kind of Incubation Period. This "Incubation" covers the time when an idea is born in an organization and stretches all the way until the beginning of the Assessment period where the project formally starts. Some project ideas are not so lucky and will never reach the Assessment period. Some can sit on a shelf for years or simply be canceled altogether. For the lucky projects that will go into production, the Incubation time can vary wildly. Sometimes critical projects can be rushed to production while others will wait until it makes sense to start them. But no matter how long the incubation period takes, basic steps should be performed before we can give the project a GO and **safely** transition into the Assessment period.

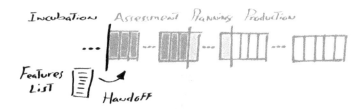

Figure 4.3 – Incubation Period and Features List

28

To set up the Scrum Team in winning conditions for the project, here is the minimal checklist for this period:

Must*
1. The vision must be described through a list of high level functionalities, requirements and objectives expected for this project. I call this the "Features List".
2. A PO that understands and believes in this vision and is ready to be dedicated to this project.

Should
3. All business stakeholders are identified and will be represented through the PO.
4. All technology stakeholders are identified and will be represented through the Dev Team.
5. The constraints from the stakeholders are clarified.
6. Dependencies or outside contributors are either resolved or the project is given the freedom to resolve issues if when synchronization becomes problematic.

Figure 3.4 – Incubation Period Checklist

The checklist for each of the periods is prioritized by numerical order (1 being the most important) and is also prioritized using MoSCoW[14]. The use of MoSCoW priorities can change between projects and organizations but here, I will sort with the generic criterias I tend to use more.

- *Must: **Show stopping** prerequisites*
- *Should: Prerequisites **impacting** the winning conditions*
- *Could: **Extra** prerequisites supporting the winning conditions*
- *Won't: this sorting level is not used*

---

[14] MoSCoW sorting method, Wikipedia, https://en.wikipedia.org/wiki/MoSCoW_method

In this "average" project, the Musts will be ensured, some compromises are expected for the Shoulds while having the Coulds would be a nice bonus. If you can use this MoSCoW sorting, your project will be off to a good start.

Before looking at each item, I have to make the distinction between the project's Features List and the constraints from the stakeholders (items 1 and 5 of the previous list). The Features List, on its own, can describe the entire project from a functionality point of view. With only this list, the PO should be able to control the entire value of the project. The stakeholders' constraints, even though they may sound bad, are very important. They help adapt the project vision to the reality of the organization, the client reality and the technology choices of the organization. That being said, stakeholders' interests are also represented in the Features List as long as they are part of the vision and are linked to the added value.

1) Largely the most important output of the incubation Period, the *Features List,* consists of a high level description of functionalities, requirements and objectives for the project which will be the roots of your Rally-Point Backlog. In this context, the definition of 'feature' is loose enough to include anything needed for the project from end-user features, admin features and purely technical items as long as this work will be done by the Dev Team. Why not stop at the user's functionalities? If you want to measure the true progress of a project, you will have to monitor the advancement of all this work anyway so why not put it all under the same measurement system? This will also question the necessity of all the 'non-feature' work by challenging its priority against the user functionalities. Some may want to go even further and think that as long as we are adding things to the Backlog, why are we not adding all the peripheral work needed for the project but not performed by the Dev Team? Doing this would create noise in the Backlog, hamper its maintenance and could impact planning. Those costs and risks are unnecessary, given that all the non-Dev Team's work can easily be tracked outside the Backlog.

In short, **the Features List should cover all the work the Dev Team will have to do to deliver this project**.

The details for this list should remain at a very high level: functionalities, features and sometimes Epics (large Stories). The amount of information should be just enough to understand the scope and complexity of the project.

2) As described previously, the project vision will fare better when carried by a strong PO. This person should completely adhere to the vision and the essence of what it tries to achieve. The PO must also be ready to work on the project and be dedicated to it until the vision is shipped.

During this Incubation period, the PO should revise the vision periodically and keep it up to date with the changing conditions. Through all those changes, the PO must stay motivated by the project. Good signs that your PO is motivated by an upcoming project are that he would be ready to start it at the drop of a hat and that he never stops selling it to you. "Just give me a team and you won't believe how cool this thing will be."

From experience, a project without minimally one "vision champion" will often be inefficient and will most likely lack team engagement. In this method, the important role of the vision champion must be played, at least in part, by the PO. As the PO is required to have a deep understanding of the project functionalities and value, it feels natural to augment what could be a clerical role into a vision leadership role.

3, 4 & 5) The stakeholders are an important part of of any project. Unless you are a one person Dev Team working on a personal project, you will have to deal with clients, coworkers or organizational guidance impacting your project. The impact of constraints may range from low to very high. It is then essential to identify all those influencers early on, deal with all their requirements and keep them updated as changes occur.

After more than 20 years in the software development business, I have yet to see a project without any constraints. During the Incubation Period, identifying as many constraints as possible is good but trying to find them all is impossible. Anybody who shipped a project knows, some of the stakeholders' constraints can only appear as the project uncovers new realities. No matter when they appear, those compulsory constraints will limit the range of options for the project and most likely affect the scope. They will need to be dealt with. Like a new ingredient in a recipe, which can impact several other ingredients in a domino effect, a new project constraint will have a multiplicative effect on the project's complexity. Because any effort invested on solving constraint issues is not spent on increasing the quality of the vision, we want to minimize those constraints. The same way the Features List should be concise, we also want the list of constraints to be as short as possible.

Some of those constraints are so important, they are invaluable for the project progression. Here are three which I try to clarify as soon as possible: the project main features, the project deadline and any constraints relative to the manpower (often the main part of the budget). The project features will dictate the Scrum Team basic composition or force an initial scoping if the necessary expertise cannot be secured. Deadline and manpower could also affect the scope, but this time from the effort capacity point of view. Getting this information and keeping it up to date is necessary for the scoping and planning effort.

Tip: Before committing to the Assessment period, I always validate with whoever is the senior technology person on the Dev Team that the budget and major delivery dates are (from a macro perspective) realistic, given the project Features List. If it feels off by a factor of 2 or more (e.g. the budget is 2 or 3 times too small), I then force either a scoping of the Features List or a review of the budget before starting the Assessment period.

This litmus test ensure that the Scrum Team has a fair chance of transforming the Features List into a Backlog that respects the budget.

6) Finally, avoid or minimize external dependencies at all cost. Of course the best outcome is to prevent this by removing the external dependency before the project starts which can be done by adding the expertise in the Dev Team. If a temporary team member is added to mitigate risk, it is a good opportunity to use this expert to train a member of the Dev Team. If unable to prevent a dependency, the best course of action is to isolate the dependency to minimize its impact on the overall effort velocity. To do so, try to concentrate the impact on a single Dev Team (when your project has more than one) or on a single developer (if you have only one Dev Team). Finally, if both methods (avoiding or isolating) are not an option, your last recourse is to reduce the overhead cost of the dependency. This can be done through tools and procedures with the aim of streamlining the coordination and communications between collaborators. Not doing anything is not an option. The cost of chaos created by an unmanaged external dependency will most likely be greater than the cost of keeping it in check. In the end, when faced with the choice between a small self-contained Agile team or a larger but distributed development force, I will always choose the smaller but predictable development capacity rather than a larger one that varies wildly.

Expiration Date
If you gathered all of the data described above, the shelf life of this work should be in the realm of mid to long term. Of course this depends on many factors, but if your Features List is not too specific and the stakeholders did not go crazy on the details, you can let this one sit on the back burner for a while. This is interesting because, unless those macro variables have changed, this work will still be relevant a few months from now and should enable you to quickly transition into the Assessment Period of this project. Having many, if not all, the potential projects in such a state of "production" readiness enables rapid project kick-offs, within days or weeks instead of months.

Transition

When transitioning between the Incubation Period into the Assessment Period, the organization not only starts a project but must also transfer a lot of control power to the PO. It must be clear to the organization and the stakeholders that, once the Assessment Period starts, the PO must be the sole person in charge of prioritizing the Backlog. This is not a one sided deal as the PO must confer with the stakeholders before making any changes to the scope. Without this full confidence and collaboration, the project will most likely veer off course as it flips and flops between outside interferences. A word of advice for the organization:

- *Staff your Dev Teams so you can trust their expertise.*
- *Select a PO so you can trust his decisions.*
- *Empower both so they can defend the business and technology needs.*

Here is a quick note on the changing dynamic at this transition stage. During the Incubation Period, the power influencing the vision is driven by strategic necessities. This power influence changes dramatically once a project starts and tactical necessities must also be accounted for.

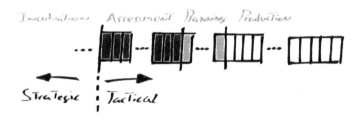

Figure 4.5 – From strategic to tactical

The strategic influence does not stop once a project starts, but it has to accommodate the tactical reality. Agile and

Scrum are designed to accept (strategic) requirement changes throughout the project and so, this power transfer to the PO does not remove the importance and influence of the stakeholders. They can still impact the project but they must act only through the PO who is standing at the intersection of the two worlds. From this unique vantage point, the PO can design solutions which will be the best compromise for the project vision, the stakeholders constraints and the Dev Team's reality. The PO might be the captain of the Backlog but the stakeholders are the admirals of the fleet.

Managing An Imperfect Transition From Incubation To Assessment

Incomplete or unclear vision
- You may not have a clear vision before crossing into the Assessment period and this can either be a bad thing or totally normal. For it to be a normal thing, it must be understood that this work will be a part of the Assessment period and, as a consequence, scope and budget may have to be revisited. So starting a project with an unclear vision can be normal but, unless you are in an art-exploration project, not pinning down the vision is a recipe for disaster.

No PO
- This is a show stopper. You must either assign a temporary PO to fill the void or delay the Assessment work until a PO is available.

A PO new to the vision or the domain
- If the PO is not an expert on the domain or the project vision, you may still go forward as long as the necessary expertise (through other people) is available to him. It is possible for a PO in this situation to manage the Backlog by value as long as he knows who to contact to get the information. It is important for the organization to support the PO by making those experts available. Communication efficiency is vital between this 'team' of collaborators for the PO.

All stakeholders are not identified or contacted
- Same as for the incomplete vision, it must be understood that, as the stakeholders are bringing in new requirements, scope and budget may have to be revisited.

Dependencies are unresolved
- As described before, unresolved outside dependencies can be handled by giving the Scrum team the freedom to manage and resolve those issues.

Now we are ready to start the project

4.3 Assessment Period

The project is officially started and we are in the first active period. During this time, the main goal is to confirm feasibility, test theories, identify and remove risks and get a general idea of what can be currently produced.

Before we go on detailing the specifics of what comprises the Assessment Period and (later on) the Planning Period, it's worth noting that both can be combined into a single period. This will depend on your organization methods or simply the size of your project. This combined period is called Inception phase[15] by Disciplined Agile and Sprint-0[16] (sprint zero) by some in the Scrum community.

Why would we want to separate these two periods? There can be many reasons for your organization to separate the Assessment from the Planning period, but what seems to be the main one is to curb development risk. When a project normally

---

[15] Disciplined Agile 2.X. *Full Agile Delivery Lifecycles*. [Online] Available at: http://www.disciplinedagiledelivery.com/lifecycle/ [Accessed 4 Mar. 2017].
[16] Prakash. A. (2013). *What Is Sprint Zero?*. [Online] Available at: https://www.scrumalliance.org/community/articles/2013/september/what-is-sprint-zero [Accessed 17 Jan. 2017].

starts, several critical unknowns remain which could reduce dramatically the value of the project. For example: (1) is the desired scope feasible for the selected team; (2) can it be done within the budget; (3) once we have considered all the constraints, can we still deliver an acceptable level of quality; (4) is this even feasible from a technology point of view? All reasonable questions for which a negative answer spells catastrophe.

To answer those questions, some organizations will allocate a [small] budget to assess the feasibility of the project and get enough information to confidently give a Go-No-Go to the project. For example, when I was working in the video game industry we would call this the Conception period (Assessment). During this time the creative team would pitch the idea for the game design while the technology team would figure out how to produce such a game. If the gameplay was good enough and possible to make, the team would get the go-ahead and proceed into pre-production (Planning). Managing a project budget this way forces the development schedule to be front-loaded with the resolution of the major unknowns. For projects of medium to large sizes, this is a good practice.

Back to our Scrum Team perspective, let's dive into the Assessment period details.

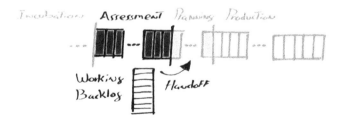

Figure 4.6 – Assessment Period and Working [Product] Backlog

As the project starts to take shape, the project vision is sometimes described by a few use cases, a list of features or a set of intentions. At the same time though, you normally have a general idea of the project scale, budget and deadline. This is the time where many developers will get nervous looking at the hazy road ahead. I was there too, but now, I have come to love this initial part of a project. This is when things get clear for the first time. For the PO, this is the starting point in a long journey where he will continuously adapt the vision while keeping it whole.

The ultimate objective of the Assessment period is to gain confidence and enough knowledge about the project to ultimately enter the Planning period and convert the vision into an actionable Backlog. To get to this level of confidence, here is the minimal checklist:

Must
1. All the known features are listed and must include all of the major features.
2. The core or the whole Dev Team is helping the PO in assessing the project.
3. All the known risks are listed or covered by the listed features.

Should
4. The budget and major delivery dates are identified or confirmed.
5. If necessary, optional features are added to manage the vision or technological risks.
6. If necessary, a preliminary scoping is done in the Features List to scale back the project within the given budget.

Could
7. If necessary, risks are removed or (minimally) clarified through prototyping.
8. All the work necessary for the Assessment period is placed in an Assessment Backlog.

Figure 4.7 – Assessment Period Checklist

1) Refining a vision into actionable work items is not simple but it must be done before starting sprint-1. Over the years, I have developed a simple rule for what this list should look like. It should contain all the known features composing the vision and they must include all core features. Here the 'core features' is what makes up the Minimum Viable Product (MVP). But why list all of the known features? Can we get away with only listing the MVP and let the rest appear during the project? In a sense, the answer is 'yes' especially if you have that luxury. On the other hand, taking the time to list all you can think of will help with the predictability of the project and, budget wise, will help calculate the estimated cost. In an Agile project, this is done through the effort estimation of the Backlog and, when building a Rally-Point Backlog using the CrumbScale estimation method, better results are rendered when the initial Backlog is a good representation of the project.

Let's address this "all the known features" statement before I get assaulted by an Agile mob. On an average project, I have found that the initial Features List describes about 80% of the final features delivered by the project. The other 20% are the details and emerging features which are always discovered during production. As long as this other 20% of features falls into the Normal work category (see chapter *Sorting the Unknowns*) it will be manageable.

Starting from the Features List created during the Incubation Period, we may have items that are unclear while other less important items, could be missing altogether. The PO must flesh out this list until it is a good representation of the known features. The level of detail for the list of features should still be high (i.e. functionalities, features or Epics), although we can sometimes see Stories appear at this point. Once the PO is done, he can now turn to the Dev Team to merge the vision and the inescapable reality of production.

2) Finally, part of the Dev Team can get on board and collaborate with the PO for the first time. Minimally, the core team should be present as their expertise and experience are necessary to assess the project from a technological point of view. The Scrum Team is now seeded and the collaboration begins with the PO presenting, or should I say 'selling', the vision of the project to the Dev Team. When possible, if I have the chance to play the PO's role, I like to invite the main stakeholders to this initial pitch. For the Dev Team, having the project's goals and constraints clearly explained by whoever the PO is representing is a plus. Presenting the vision to the Dev Team is the first step toward engaging them in the project.

Killing two birds with the same stone, I like to use this initial meeting of the Scrum Team as an opportunity to further engage the Dev Team while opening the door to innovation. This is done by starting an open discussion about the project and brainstorming ideas on how to deliver it or, even, make it better.

3) The Features List is now covering all the major features composing the vision. By looking at those features the team should be able to uncover the major risks of the project and complete the feature definitions by detailing those risks. If a new risk is identified but can not be related to a feature, you should strongly doubt the necessity of adding on this risk. Remember that risk can sometimes be related to a project constraint. Linking all the work to tangible features (simultaneously linking it to the project value) will help the PO and stakeholders understand its importance.

Again, the level of detail when describing the risks should still be high. At this point of the project, we only need to know that the risk exists and that it is possible for the Dev Team to handle it during the production iterations.

4) Depending on how you manage project budgeting you may already know your budget and delivery dates before the project starts. Sometimes, this information will be defined or need to be gathered during the Assessment Period. This may sound simple but it impacts every aspect of the project. Here are the kind of questions that should be answered once we know the budget and delivery dates:

- Can we afford all the necessary expertise?
- How many sprints will the Dev Team have?
- Will the team members be dedicated at 100% on the project? If not, what will be the capacity for each team member?
- How many deliveries are planned and what content do we expect?
- How many demos are planned?
- Can we afford the necessary equipment?
- If applicable, are the external project collaborators aligned with this budget and dates?

5) A truly Agile Backlog can survive major setbacks both on the vision side and on the technical side. When possible, critical features should have 2-3 design solutions ranging from the optimal version, a simple version and a bare minimum version. In the same way, the architecture and technical solutions should have 2-3 approaches ranging from the best coding choices down to a quick and dirty version. This level of flexibility is not easy to achieve but it is an insurance policy giving you room to maneuver when facing the critical moments of the project. I call this having a **variable geometry vision** and a **variable geometry architecture**.

Practically this means you may have 2-3 stories for the same feature in your Backlog and all of them should be estimated in effort points. This may look like a lot of work but if it is done only for the main features and estimated using the CrumbScale effort estimation method (see section *5.3 Step 2: CrumbScale Points Distribution*) it can be done rapidly. When handling a Backlog content this way, it goes without saying that (by design) many stories will remain untouched at the end of the project. To keep all those extra stories organized in such a way that planning is not a problem, the best approach is to rate the stories with MoSCoW. One way of sorting is to have Must stories defining the MVP, the Should stories defining the normal features and the Could stories defining the extra (nice to have) features. This way you can plan a worst case scenario using the Must and a best case using the Should or Could.

Taking the time to create this level of flexibility in your Backlog is one of the best ways to ensure shipping a project. As Joel Spolsky wrote in his blog; 'shipping is a feature'[17]. It was his way of explaining why it is better to ship a partial solution than to never ship a perfect solution. A variable geometry vision and architecture generates most of the leverage I need as a PO to ship a working solution, partial or not.

6) Finally, as all the other Assessment steps are being done, the project scope is continuously revised by the PO, adapting it in real time as new information is pouring in. This is true for many Agile projects where budget and time are decided before the start of the Assessment period leaving scope as the only flexible part. On the other hand, if your organization uses the Assessment Period to finalise the understanding of the project vision and its production cost, this opens the door for a holistic approach to innovation and problem solving as budget, time and scope are adapted at the same time.

To get this level of design flexibility, communication is key. Mainly, the communication of information between the Dev Team and the stakeholders, since now that the project is officially started, direct and instantaneous communication is not always smooth if even possible. Still, as new information about risks and constraints is uncovered, propositions and discussions involving the stakeholders must take place and converge toward

---

[17] Spolsky. J. (2009). *The Duct Tape Programmer*. [Online] Available at: https://www.joelonsoftware.com/2009/09/23/the-duct-tape-programmer/ [Accessed 23 Jan. 2017].

the right mix of features, resources and release dates until a plan is agreed upon. This is sadly where many projects fail. How does the Rally-Point Backlog resolve this?

This is where the central role of the [Rosetta] Backlog and the leadership role of the PO comes into play. The goal here is to always keep the stakeholders in the loop regarding constraints found by the Dev Team and, of course, to always keep the Dev Team in the loop regarding constraints found by the stakeholders. Then, we must have a way to go back and forth between the two groups as a compromise is defined. To do so, from this point on, the PO must act as a mediator between the stakeholders' world and the Dev Team's world. Each new constraint must be resolved, reflected in the Backlog and agreed upon by both the stakeholders and the Dev Team. Here are the communication loops to make this happen:

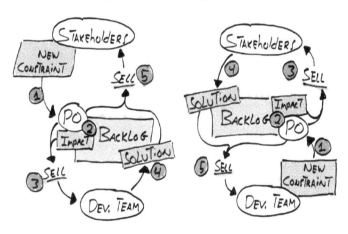

Figure 4.8 – Backlog Collaboration Loops

The two loops are almost identical with the exception of the delegation level regarding the control of the Backlog. This is necessary since the Backlog must remain a collaborative work between the PO and the Dev Team. For the sake of clarity, I use here the terminology of the Seven Levels of Delegation[18]. When

---

[18] Management 3.0 Practice: Delegation Board, [online] Available at:

interacting with the stakeholders, the PO maximizes collaboration while keeping control over the Backlog integrity by **consulting** with them. On the other hand, when interacting with the Dev Team, the PO maximizes collaboration while maintaining the Backlog integrity by reaching **agreements** with them.

Let's look at the two possible scenarios pictured in Figure 4.8. In the first scenario, a new constraint is found on the stakeholders' side. First, the PO **consults** with the stakeholders to find how the Backlog could be modified (impacted) in order to meet the new constraint. The PO must then sell this new stakeholders' constraint to the Dev Team by clarifying the difference between what is minimally expected vs. the best case scenario where value is maximized. Then, the PO works with the Dev Team to find a working solution they can **agree** upon. Finally, the PO returns to the stakeholders and explains [sells] the selected solution and how it respects the initial constraint.

In the second scenario, a new constraint is found on the Dev Team's side. First, the PO **agrees** with the Dev Team to find how the Backlog could be modified (impacted) to meet the new constraint. The PO must then sell this new Dev Team's constraint to the stakeholders by clarifying the difference between what is minimally needed vs. the best case scenario where risk is minimized. Then, the PO **consults** with the stakeholders as they pick from the proposed solutions. Finally, the PO returns to the Dev Team and explains [sells] the selected solution and the reasoning behind the decision.

Sometimes, the PO will have to go around the loop a second time for minor tweaks on the solution, but avoid at all costs turning this into an endlessly spinning nightmare. Keep in mind that the Backlog must always come back into a clean state where it represents the current reality of the vision and technology. It must remain the single source of truth.

https://management30.com/practice/delegation-board/ [Accesed 8 Jan 2017].

7) Risk is the dangerous stuff that can derail your project. Yet, without risk, nothing new would be created and so we try to take as much risk as possible without losing control. Also, risks are often linked to the most valuable features of a project and can not be easily dismissed. The main tool, for the Dev Team, for removing risk during the Assessment Period is through prototyping. Coming back to the concept of an Assessment Backlog (see item #8 in this checklist), all the work needed for the different prototypes should be maintained in the Assessment Backlog and, if necessary, carried into the Planning Period or even the Production Period. Risk being an important subject, I will get back to it in the following section *5 Sorting the Unknowns*.

8) At some point in the Assessment Period, I also introduce the concept of an *Assessment Backlog* in which the team will put all the work needed for the Assessment and Planning periods. This Assessment Backlog will be the team's todo list as they move toward the creation of the actual Backlog. Naturally, being Agile and all, the team can do sprints using this Assessment Backlog but it is not an obligation. If you do, my personal preference is to have 1 week sprints. This enables the Dev Team to keep pace as much as possible with the evolving situation while they are learning more and more about the reality of the project. Sprinting also helps the team maintain good Scrum habits and not fall into a chaotic mess where everyone is running around without common focus. Another advantage of having an Assessment Backlog is that it will turn out to be the seed for the actual Backlog. The Dev Team will identify and start different work during both the Assessment and the Planning periods and, almost every single time, some of this work will be either in progress or untouched at the beginning of Sprint-1. Without an Assessment Backlog turning into a Backlog, all this work has a tendency to stay up in the air and is often represented by a bunch of aging sticky notes around the developers' screens. This unfinished technical debt can linger and take the evil form of 'side work' eroding the team's capacity over one or many sprints. To avoid that, we roll over the relevant content of the Assessment Backlog into the Backlog just before the point estimation activity, while the team is merging the Technical Stories with the Business Stories. Now joined into a single list, all those elements can be prioritized against each other helping the PO understand and manage their impact. Just like the pure Technical Stories, the business value of such Backlog elements can be calculated by the impact of not doing them.

With the introduction of the Assessment Backlog concept, we can now see the different forms the vision takes as it progresses from an early concept to a production-ready Rally-Point Backlog.

1. Strategic Vision (during the Incubation Period)
   1.1. Concept
   1.2. Features List & Constraints
2. Tactical Vision (during and after the Assessment Period)
   2.1. Assessment Backlog
   2.2. Backlog

Expiration Date
The normal shelf life for all the work done during an Assessment Period is hovering between short to medium while leaning toward short. The reasons to avoid wasting time and swiftly carry on to the Planning Period are plenty. The Dev Team is already engaged in the project, and their work environment (both physical and virtual) may already be partially set up. The Assessment Backlog may also have important work in it that is only relevant to this Dev Team at this particular time. Waiting 2 to 3 months between the Assessment and the Planning periods will most probably cost you a loss in momentum (since you will likely need to revisit work done in the Assessment period) and a drop in team engagement. Try to avoid a delay between these two periods if you can.

Transition

During the transition between the Assessment and the Planning period the PO must, unless it is already done, share some project ownership by collaborating with the Dev Team, working toward the creation of the Backlog. This collaboration effort often is the first 'full' collaboration moment involving the PO and the Dev Team and will define their relationship for the whole project.

Managing An Imperfect Transition From Assessment To Planning

Incomplete Features List
- If this is caused by an unclear vision, it must be understood that clarifying the vision will be a part of the Planning and, most probably, the Production period. As a consequence, scope and budget will most likely be revisited during those periods. If this is clear with all the stakeholders then you can move forward. Avoid starting a project with an unclear vision and managing it as if it had one. That would be a recipe for disaster.
- If this is caused by the lack of expertise to turn the vision into a list of features, it is a big issue at this stage of the process. The Assessment period was the last responsible time to assemble a project core team with the combined necessary expertise to adapt the vision. Without all of the core expertise, the Scrum Team will not be able to adapt the vision, estimate the Backlog, execute the project and gain predictability. In such a situation, staff accordingly and extend the Assessment Period as needed.

The Features List was created without the core Dev Team
- The Assessment Period is when the business vision meets with the Dev Team reality for the first time and the most effective way to do so is to have the core Dev Team work with the PO. Until this is properly done, the vision will not be adapted to the reality of the project and thus not ready for a predictable execution. It might not even make it through the estimation process as the

Dev Team will have to contend with an unadapted set of features, resulting in many of the features being considered risks. This can be resolved by the PO presenting the Features List to the Dev Team and working in collaboration to adapt the problematic features.

Known risks are not covered in the Features List

- This may happen if the technological risks are not included (or described) in the Features List. Some of the technology risk may not relate on a one to one basis with one of the business features. In such a case it still must be added to the Features List (minimally as a technical constraint) in order to be carried into the Backlog.

- Failing to list all of the known features in the Features List may hide what would be known risks. Unmanaged risk can prevent predictability and cost features or even derail the project. The simple fix is to list all of the known features and review them, looking for possible risks.

No budget or due date

- Lucky you, you may be in one of those awesome organizations that starts a project by saying "Here's what we want, now tell us how much it will cost.". The Assessment period can then be used to calculate the ideal budget to deliver the Features List. This not being an open bar, it is good form to propose more than one scenario ranging from best case (all the features) to worst case (only the MVP) with their associated budgets.

- In the case where the budget is critical but not available, simply pause the Assessment and wait for the info. Without the budget to limit the available options, the team may waste valuable time doing adaptation work only to throw it out or redo it later. This is wasteful money-wise, and also not good for the team morale. Some work might still be doable in such a scenario, but be careful.

No optional features

- This is not a show stopper but you are losing an opportunity of giving extra flexibility to the Backlog. This type of flexibility is also an insurance policy to protect predictability as it gives options to the PO when faced with change.

Features List not scoped

- Scoping can be done later, once the Backlog is estimated and an initial planning is done. The cost of not pre-scoping the Features List is that the Scrum Team will carry those extra features into the Backlog, probably transform them into Stories, estimate, prioritize and plan them, after which they may be scoped out of the Backlog. This extra work is time not used on creating value and may be wasted if those features are indeed scoped out or simply not executed during the project. It is better to scope the Features List and, if necessary, re-introduce a scoped out feature later on during the project if it suddenly becomes important. The work of adding it into the Backlog will then be pertinent.

Risk remains in the Backlog

- As long as the risk in the Backlog is acceptable and is not a threat to predictability it is OK to leave it there. Some bad risks at this point would be:
  - Risk in the MVP features
  - Risk preventing the estimation of the Backlog
  - Risk outside of the Dev Team expertise
  - Too much risk

No Assessment Backlog

- Not having an Assessment Backlog is not a problem but any remaining work from the Assessment period will have to be carried into the Planning period so that it is not forgotten.

We now have just enough information to start planning.

4.4 Planning Period

This is it. The last blitz of preparation before the production iterations can start. If done right, committing the team in the sequence of events of the Planning Period will cement the Scrum Team's engagement in the project. It will also shift the team's focus from preparation to production. Then again, this new state of mind will not last long unless you dive right away into Sprint-1 and immerse the team into the daily life of production. Think of it as the last pep talk of the coach before a sport team gets on the field. This pep talk would not have the same effect if given a week before the event.

In the Scrum world this period (often called Sprint-0) is use for finalizing the Backlog, estimating it in effort points[19], and prioritizing it in order to be ready for Sprint-1. Also, if you apply the CrumbScale method (described in the next chapter *5 Product Backlog – A Team Effort*), the Planning Period will also give you an initial effort velocity enabling you to take a first step toward predictability.

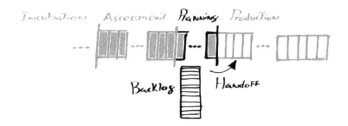

Figure 4.9 – Planning Period and Backlog

Deceptively short and simple looking, the importance of this period is often underestimated. Other than creating and estimating the Backlog, other steps must happen in order to produce a meaningful and predictable Backlog. Depending on how much was done during the Assessment period, the amount of work may range from the full creation of the Backlog to only

---

[19] e.g. Story Points or CrumbScale Points

doing minor tweaks and going straight to points estimation. Keeping things straightforward, we will continue where the Assessment Period left off.

For the PO, the Planning Period is an important time to complete the adaptation of the vision with the current capabilities of technology. More specifically, to the technological capabilities of the actual Dev Team that will be delivering this project. Once the production iterations are on the way, adaptation will still occur but with far less flexibility and at a much greater cost. This action or "adapting the vision" can sometimes scare the organization as it is perceived as a loss of control over the project vision. On the contrary, this is the ultimate failsafe to validate the project feasibility and scope. Sure the project may have looked "feasible" when estimated with a generic Dev Team in mind but now this is reality. This is the one team that will execute the project.

Look at it this way, if the Dev Team is staffed properly, you have nothing to worry about. They should have the right expertise and manpower to deliver the project. If so, the technological capabilities of the Dev Team should not force any surprising adaptation of the vision. On the other hand, if the team's composition or strength is not a perfect match, you want to know this as early as possible. Like the saying goes "Fail early, fail often". If you miss this chance, and indeed there is a mismatch between the vision and the team's capabilities, the vision will be adapted anyway but forcefully this time, as the PO will have to do it during the iterations and armed with much less options.

Rant
Think of your team's capabilities the same as their happiness level. When times are tough, you may really, really, realllllly want them to be having fun but you just can't force happiness. At any given moment, the team's morale (or happiness level) is the result of all preceding events, organization culture and the mix of personalities. It takes time to build and tweak all those moving parts into a safe and productive group. Building

an effective team is hard. Happiness is not a task and cannot be ordered spontaneously. Technological capabilities (skills) are the same in the way in which they take time to build up and take continuous work to maintain. Still, some people believe in forcing happiness onto people and thus think this argument is moot. Such people have much bigger problems than trying to build a Backlog.

Adding yet another layer of complexity, the limit of a team's technical capabilities is not a well known line but a fuzzy border which can be positively or negatively impacted by environmental factors. By working in close proximity with the Dev Team, the PO will learn which section of this fuzzy border is easier or safer to challenge. And so, not surprisingly, a fully engaged team in a collaborative environment where the vision is ready to work with the team's strengths, will be able to stretch its limits further. With this in mind, let's look at the minimal checklist needed to create a Backlog and get it ready for Sprint-1:

Must
1. The PO and the Dev Team transforms the Features List into Stories and Epics (including technical Stories).
2. The engagement of the PO and the Dev Team is secured.
3. The Dev Team estimates the Story effort in points.
4. The PO prioritizes the Backlog by value.

Should
5. The Dev Team prepares their *Definition of Done.*
6. The Dev Team does the first sprint planning which reveals the initial effort velocity estimate.
7. The PO plans the deliverable(s) based on the initial effort velocity and re-prioritizes the Backlog if necessary, always keeping a 15-20% buffer.

Could
8. The PO adds business values to each Story and Epic.

Figure 4.10 – Planning Period Checklist

In the next chapter *5 Product Backlog – A Team Effort*, the Crumbscale Backlog creation method will cover all but one item in this list (point 8). Of course, you can deliver the content of this checklist by using any Agile methodology you desire, but for the sake of shameless self promotion, keep in mind that CrumbScale Backlog was specifically created to optimize this process.

1) Very often, this is the first time the full Scrum Team is working together. Unless this full team took part in the Assessment Period, the PO must kick things off by presenting the vision and the Features List to the Dev Team. As mentioned before, the word 'presenting' is not strong enough since the PO must actually 'sell' this vision to the Dev Team to ensure a deep understanding of the intent. It goes without saying that the PO must himself be engaged in the project before trying to sell it to anyone. After the vision is well understood, the PO and Dev Team proceed with the translation of each Feature into a Story and/or Epic. One by one the Features are presented to the Dev Team by the PO and, together, they write the Stories and Epics necessary to deliver them. To do this, the team can use any method they want. Personally, I often use a variation on the popular Story Mapping[20] method. It is important to aim at creating self-contained Vertical Stories[21] delivering value-added functionalities to the end user. This is not always possible and some purely *technical stories*[22] may appear from time to time. Those technical stories are normally prerequisites for one or more Stories and this dependency must not be lost in the Backlog.

As the team works together, to extract the most value out of this collaboration, compromises must be made by both the PO and the Dev Team. The PO must sometimes make tweaks to

---

[20] *Story Mapping*. [Online] Available at:
https://www.agilealliance.org/glossary/storymap/ [Accessed 26 Feb. 2017]
[21] Kremik. N. Horizontal and Vertical User Stories - Slicing the Cake. [Online] Available at: http://www.deltamatrix.com/horizontal-and-vertical-user-stories-slicing-the-cake/ [Accessed 26 Feb. 2017]
[22] Also known as Non-Functional Requirements or NFR

PHILLIPE CANTIN

the vision to avoid a technical risk. On the other hand, the Dev Team must also adjust their approach to accommodate better solutions for the vision. This is where the vision must stay open and get inspired by the technology while the technology must accept to be challenged by the vision.

2) During this entire process, it is essential to always protect the vision and keep everybody engaged. If it is done right, when all the features are turned into Stories, the whole team can take a look at the Backlog and feel confident that it represents the project's reality. This will pump them up as they are getting ready for the next step. Take the time to ensure that this is the case and, if needed, make the necessary adjustments in the Backlog.

3) This step can be done with any of the popular effort estimation methods using points. But for me, when using the CrumbScale method, this is my favorite part of a project start. Assuming it is done using CrumbScale, this step normally takes around 1 hour per 30-60 stories. For example the first time I experimented with this method, my team and I estimated a Backlog of around 300 items in 4 hours. Results may vary depending on how well the Dev Team understands the Backlog items. What was taking weeks when estimating in man-hours, and days when estimating in Poker Planning, will now take you a few hours. So, yeah, CrumbScale for the win!

4) Now that each Story and Epic in the Backlog has an effort point, the PO can order the Backlog to maximize the value. Doing this step after the points estimation significantly helps the PO with prioritization. It can prevent having only large (effort wise) stories at the top of the Backlog before the sprint planning. It can also help separate by effort size, stories which from a functionality of business value perspective, look identical. It can also trigger a dialog between the PO and the Dev Team as to why a certain Story costs so much and another costs so little. This, again, will help close the gap between the PO and the Dev Team as the PO gains more information about the fuzzy borders of their technological capabilities.

As a last precaution, we sometimes have dependencies between stories and it is therefore important to validate the final ordering with the Dev Team. In a way, one could say that the Dev Team controls the *Technical sub-Order* of the Backlog while the PO has complete control over the overall *Value Order*.

5) After having listed all the Stories but before the points estimation exercise, the Dev Team must agree on their common *Definition of Done* (DOD). The DOD has a huge influence on the points estimation by providing the Dev Team with a common understanding of the necessary steps to be considered. It is also recommended to define (or, if it already exists, review) the DOD after the Stories are created, while the entire project is fresh in the minds of the Dev team.

6 & 7) It is now time for the team to dive into the first Sprint Planning. Nothing fancy, just a normal sprint planning, except this is the sprint planning for Sprint-1 even though we are still in the Planning Period. The idea here is to be as rigorous as you normally are and, starting from the top of the Backlog, take the Stories into your Sprint Backlog until it is full (or 85% full if you are a fan of Queuing Theory[23]). Once this is done you can add up the points (from the stories that made it into the sprint Backlog) and, voila!, you have your initial velocity value before sprint-1 even started. I normally try to get this Sprint-1 planning done 2-3 days before the end of the Planning Period, leaving time for the PO to plan with this initial effort velocity.

8) The PO must now specify a business value for each item in the Backlog. I won't go into the details of this process since any method that works for you will do just fine and should

---

[23] In Queuing theory (https://en.wikipedia.org/wiki/Queueing_theory), when looking at the Latency Curve created from the queue response time vs utilisation, the response will increase sharply near a utilisation of 70% to 85% creating a threshold (or knee). This is the maximum point beyond which the queue efficiency is decreasing rapidly as the response time is grow exponentially.

not impact the rest of the Backlog creation. Even though it is important for the project as a whole, this step is left out of the CrumbScale method since it has no impact on gaining predictability of the effort velocity. On the other hand, adding value information to the Backlog stories is essential to understanding the progress of the project from a business value perspective instead of simply tracking when each feature will be delivered. Sometimes you may want to stop a project when specific stories are completed (e.g. all the MVP stories), or you may stop the project based on how much value points were delivered no matter which stories they come from.

Expiration Date

The resulting Backlog is now ready for production sprints. Starting Sprint-1 as soon as possible is now critical since many fine details in the Backlog will only be meaningful for a short time. In reality I would not let a team go into this type of Planning Period unless I'm also ready to let them continue into sprint-1. Engagement wise, since the team has been through the process of planning sprint-1, they normally are primed to start, and morale could take a hit if we stall them. Unless the initial velocity value is a complete disaster or something dramatic is changing the project, just go for it and start sprint-1 ASAP.

Transition

Contrary to the two previous transitions, passing from Planning to Production is not about delegating or sharing power, but all about changing the work dynamic. Coming back to the athlete's analogy, this would be like transitioning from training mode to competition mode. During training you do all kinds of things to get ready for competition time but when the competition starts your mind is on one thing only and you cannot be interrupted.

Getting into production mode, understanding the new reality of a project, and stabilizing your velocity is a lot of work. It takes a lot of effort to get the team in the productivity zone (i.e. flow[24]) and the last thing you want is to get them out of "the

56

zone". In short, organize the team during the Assessment Period, focus them during the Planning Period and release them into the Production Period with the intent of keeping them in this state until the project is complete. You don't stop a marathon runner mid race to try on a pair of shoes from a new sponsor. Scrum sprinting is a mind set. Don't break the focus.

Managing An Imperfect Transition From Planning to Production

All the features are not represented in the Backlog
- To be a true Rally-Point Backlog, the Backlog must become and remain the best representation of the project. This cannot be the case if all the features are not listed in it. This is the first step of the Planning Period and the Scrum Team cannot move forward without doing it. Extend the Planning period as necessary to complete this task.

The PO is not engaged in the project
- The PO may not be supported or trusted by the organization. Trusting, supporting and protecting the PO is fundamental to the Rally-Point Backlog (and Scrum in general). This is a show stopper and it must be resolved. If the problem is a bad PO, change him. If you have a good PO, protect him by changing the culture around him. If this is a junior PO, have him coached or mentored.
- This may be caused by a poor relationship between the PO and the stakeholders. The PO, with the support of the organization, should mend this relationship as it is critical to keep the alignment between the business needs and the project reality.
- The PO may also have problems creating a good link with the Dev Team. To collaborate well with the Dev Team, the PO must be present (available), be able to sell them the project vision, and respect their expertise.

---

[24] Flow (psychology), also known as the zone. wikipedia.org, https://en.wikipedia.org/wiki/Flow_(psychology)

At the same time the Dev Team must accept the PO's expertise on the vision and also be engaged in the project.
- The Scrum Master can help the PO develop his collaboration channels.
- In an impasse, finding a new PO that believes in the vision and works well with both the stakeholders and the Dev Team might also be the solution.

The Dev Team is not engaged in the project
- The Dev Team may not be trusted by the organization. Trusting the Dev Team is fundamental to the Rally-Point Backlog (and Scrum in general). This is a show stopper and it must be resolved. Staff the Dev Team properly and/or change the culture around them.
- This may be caused by a poor relationship between the Dev Team and the PO. The Dev Team, with the support of the SM, should mend this relationship as it is critical to keep the alignment between the development reality and the business needs.
- The PO may need to include the Dev Team more in the adaptation of the vision.
- Leadership in the Dev Team may not be adequate (both Morale Leadership and Technical leadership).

The Backlog is not estimated
- Well… just do it then. Moving forward without this important step will prevent predictability.

The Backlog is not prioritized
- Sprint-1 cannot start without this important step.

No definition of done
- Without a basic definition of done, the effort estimation of the Backlog will take longer and be less precise. This imprecision may in turn affect predictability. The Dev Team should take the time to create a basic definition of done before the initial Backlog effort estimation.

No planning
- Planning will influence prioritization, but if unable to do it during the Planning period, it is necessary to complete it during Sprint-1, before the sprint planning for Sprint-2.

No business value on the Backlog items
- This step can be replaced by other methods of managing the value of the Backlog items (e.g. MoSCoW combined with prioritization).
- This step can also be completed during the first couple of Sprints.

The vision is now properly translated into a Rally-Point Backlog and the project can switch into execution mode by moving into the Production Period.

4.5 Production Period

You finally made it to the starting line. You have all the pieces of the puzzle in place and the team can start production iterations. They will stay in this mode until either the project's goals are achieved or as long as the effort velocity remains predictable.

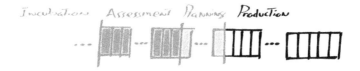

Figure 4.11 – Production Period

If we look at this period from a Backlog creation perspective, one may think that there is nothing left to say. Sure, stories will be tweaked, added and removed as the project moves along but there are cases where the Backlog will need more than tweaking. If one or more unknowns (on the vision side or the technical side) disturb the Backlog so much that velocity is destabilized and predictability is lost, the team may be forced to stop sprinting and regroup by doing a new planning period. This extra planning period would be fueled by new information the team collected during the preceding sprints. The resulting Backlog would reflect the readjusted vision taking full consideration of the problematic unknowns. As an example, imagine a project where, after 2-3 sprints, the team discovers a show stopper limitation and does not have enough flexibility (choices) in the current Backlog to correct the situation. The team could then fall back into a short Assessment/Planning Period, define a new approach, add the necessary stories to the Backlog, estimate their effort in points, prioritize and come back into production mode. This extreme measure should not be taken lightly but sometimes it is better to fall back and regroup than to keep on beating a dead horse.

While reading the list of work needed for each period, you may have had flashbacks of previous projects where many of those steps were skipped or not even considered. More often than not, as the project relentlessly moved forward, such mistakes would remain uncorrected and their impact simply pushed forward as extra work, added stress and unnecessary risks. Then again, perfection rarely goes hand in hand with software development projects. Mistakes will happen and necessary steps will remain unfinished. When they do, it is possible to control their impact during the transition time with a mixture of respect, empowerment and scoping.

5 Product Backlog - A Team Effort

*There's that point when you just finish the first
sprint planning of a brand new Product
Backlog, the point where the fog clears for the
first time and you see the reality of the project in
front of you. To me this moment feels like being
at the base of a mountain knowing that you have
all the right gear, all the abilities to reach the
top and the confidence that nothing can stop
you. For an instant, the clouds part just enough
to get a glimpse of the summit.*

Screenplay writers avoid creating single purpose scenes. With a
little care, each moment can be used to move the plot forward,
develop a character, build relationships or introduce a new twist.
In the same fashion, every Scrum event, meeting, sprint,
deliverable or project period is an opportunity to clarify the
vision, remove risk, engage the team, improve and ship a
concrete part of the project. As the major artifact of the Scrum
framework, the Product Backlog (Backlog) is a solid anchor to
which we can attach a multitude of purposes.

5.1 METHOD 2: *CrumbScale Backlog*

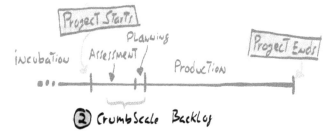

Figure 5.1 – Method 2 in relation to the project timeline

In that same spirit of multi purpose, Creating a CrumbScale Backlog will add two functions to the the well known Scrum Backlog: maximizing the chances of gaining predictability, and systematically engaging the Scrum Team in the project. To build such a Backlog, the CrumbScale method covers the Backlog creation process from the initial breakdown of features into Stories, through the assignment of effort points, and ends with the initial prioritization and planning. As this is done, an added benefit of using this method will be the creation of a fast estimation tool, simply called the CrumbScale, which will be used for all future estimations during the Production Period.

How will CrumbScale achieve those two things? Predictability will mostly come from controlling the Backlog content and the use of the CrumbScale effort estimation method. Engagement, on the other hand, will come from the systematic collaborative approach of adapting the project vision to the technology reality, culminating in the creation of the CrumbScale Backlog. As described in the chapter *3 Road To Rally-Point*, the Backlog stands at the exact center of the project where the frontier between vision and technology lies. With this in mind we will build a Backlog both the Product Owner (PO) and the Development Team (Dev Team) can trust to represent their reality.

Enough overview. Pragmatically speaking, to achieve all this, the CrumbScale Backlog needs to end up with the following characteristics:

- Contains the known functionalities in the form of Stories or Epics
- Must cover all of the 'Must Have' features
- All of the known risks are addressed
- The effort for each Story and Epic is estimated in points
- Prioritized by value by the PO
- Basic planning is done and, if necessary, scoping too

Figure 5.2 – Basic characteristics of a CrumbScale Backlog*

Here, the overlap with the Handle it or hand it over method is pretty clear. See Figure 4.7 and 4.10

Estimation using points (points estimation) and effort velocity predictability is central to this method and the first three items in this list are fundamental requisites. In the interest of simplicity, the finer explanations of the mechanics underpinning CrumbScale are explained in a later chapter (*8 ANNEX - How CrumbScale Works*). For now, let's say the the first three items are there to ensure that we have a good reliable set of data on which to base our predictions. With this out of the way, we can dive into the method without stopping every three paragraphs for some ever-so-exciting information on math, statistics and cognitive biases.

Some of you will have also noticed that I did not mention the assignment of business value in this list. This is done on purpose since it has no effect on this method's goals of predictability and engagement. The main impact of adding value information will be to help prioritize the Backlog and monitor the delivery of value which does not correlate with effort velocity. To be clear, monitoring business value is an important part of an Agile project though, as far as predictability goes, in a software development project, the effort velocity can be stabilized enough to reliably support planning while the value velocity can not. Even if you have a perfect Agile/Scrum scenario (which I have never seen), and all your stories are equal-sized self-contained deliverable functionalities (which I have never seen), stabilizing the business value velocity on a sprint by sprint basis is not likely to happen. Luckily, if the two concepts of "effort velocity" and "value point monitoring" are combined together, the predictability of the effort velocity will help forecast the business value delivery. On with the Backlog making.

First things first, some pieces must be in place before we can start building a Backlog. People-wise, we need the PO (who has all the expertise necessary to understand the stakeholders' needs and constraints) and the Dev Team (who has all the expertise necessary to understand the production's needs and constraints). Input wise, we need the PO's Features List (in Spreadsheet form is highly recommended), and the Dev Team's *Definition of Done.* Location and tool wise, we need a room with seats for everyone and a projector (or big screen). It is always good to also have a table and a whiteboard even though those are not required by this method. Yes, when creating a CrumbScale Backlog, the prefered tool is a spreadsheet like Excel®, LibreOffice Calc or Google Sheets and the use of a projector in order for the whole group to see. The main reasons for using a spreadsheet instead of sticky notes are scalability and speed. CrumbScale was designed to scale for large Backlogs of 300+ items and the estimation process goes too fast to be handled through sticky notes. Also, having the Features and Stories already in an electronic format will speed up the process of transferring the results in the Agile software of your choice.

Point of no return
The next step will commit the whole team to the project. This is the starting line of a series of actions that can only end by launching you into Sprint-1 and the project Production Period. "Why is that?" you may ask. The short answer is this: building a Backlog is like the pep-talk before the match. As we get through the pep-talk, morale is rising and people get pumped up until they are prime to get started. The pep-talk is also very specific, as it is meant for this team at this exact moment in time. You don't do a pep-talk one month before a game and you don't use generic information that could fit any

team at any moment. It is the same for building a CrumbScale Backlog. If you make the Backlog now it will only be meaningful for the current PO, the current development team(s), and this, for a short period of time. If you switch the PO, the vision described in the Backlog will likely be confusing to the new PO and it will take time and tweaks for him to master it. If you you switch the Dev Team, the points estimation will be lost and the technology choices described in the Backlog will most likely be incompatible with the new Dev Team. If you wait before starting the project, the vision, the technologies, the constraints and the team's expertise will most likely change. This in turn, will make the Backlog content out of date and the team might be forced to rebuild and re-estimate the whole thing. As you can see, a false start will waste time and, based on experience, damage the team's morale. Make sure you are ready before you engage your team in this step.

5.2 Step 1: From Features to Stories

Think of building a Backlog as a series of rapid radar passes enabling you to look at everything at least once. At each pass, the goal is to spot the big ticket items that need more detailing, identify the potential risks and split massive work items until they feel small enough to be Epics or Stories.

Figure 5.3 – The initial ingredients

Features List and Constraints

The raw material you need to start creating a Backlog is the *Features List* which, as described by this method, could contain features but also requirements, constraints and use cases. We aim to build a Backlog containing the known functionalities, covering 100% of the Musts and the known risks. This Features List must give us enough information to do so. On the other hand, building this original list is not a precise science. There will always be unknowns and unexpected difficulties popping up during production, continuously forcing you to adapt your plan. Still, insuring that you have the known requirements, constraints and risks when creating the initial Backlog will lay down a foundation solid enough to start building on it.

Presenting to the team

Adapting vision to reality is done in two phases: the first phase happens during the Backlog creation (covered in this book), while the second one occurs during the Production Period as the chaos of development is hitting every sprint. Focusing on the first phase, we initiate this 'merging' of vision with the Dev Team's expertise when the PO explains the project's context and goals. In the case of bigger projects, the PO may be accompanied by other stakeholders who can help explain the context of the project. In the end though, the PO must come across as 'in charge' and in control of the Backlog. The leadership and salesmanship qualities of the PO are crucial during this initial contact with the team and the project and, if done right, it will empower the team to carry on through the many obstacles to come. From experience, an empowered team included at such an early step has a tendency to take more risks and push the project further. This contrasts with a team that is onboarded later, once the Stories are defined, the technology decisions have been taken and the team is only asked to execute (somebody else's) work.

> *"If you have a good idea and you give it to a mediocre group, they'll screw it up. If you give a mediocre idea to a good group, they'll fix it or they'll throw it away and come up with something else."*[25]
>
> - Ed Catmull

It is essential that this presentation is given to, minimally, the core Dev Team which will later on take part in the points estimation. If the whole Dev Team is not present, this core group must represent them well. They must be respected ambassadors and influencers trusted by the rest of the Dev Team so that they can explain and *sell* all the technology decisions that were taken in their absence. This important step will engage the remaining team members into the project. On the other hand, omitting to do so will create a divide between the "engaged" core team and the second group simply in "execution" mode.

Collaborative Creation of Stories

Once the vision of the project is understood by the Dev Team, they can help the PO break down the features into what we will call Business Stories. There are many existing methods

---

[25] Catmull. E. (2007). *Keep Your Crises Small*. [Online video] Available at: https://www.youtube.com/watch?v=k2h2lvhzMDc [Accessed 5 Jan. 2017].

to do so and, as mentioned previously, my preferred method is Story Mapping, but you can use whatever you are comfortable with as long as it is done collaboratively with the whole Scrum Team and all the features are transformed into Stories.

During and after this activity, as the Business Stories are defined, the Dev Team will inevitably come up with Technical Stories needed, here and there, to support the development of the Business Stories. Initially, those Technical Stories will look and feel like a bunch of prerequisites and it will be important not to leave the Backlog in this state. Prerequisite stories can render the PO powerless by interlocking all the Stories and preventing prioritization by business value. To minimize the impact of the Technical Stories, we need to combine them as much as possible with the original Business Stories using methods like the following ones:

1. Combine Technical Stories into existing PO's Stories by merging their definitions.
2. Splitting PO's Stories into 2 or more smaller feature increments.
3. Combine Technical Stories together into new feature increments.
4. Add or eliminate Business Stories as needed.
5. Leave a Technical Story as a prerequisite for selected PO's Stories.

Figure 5.4 – Methods for merging Technical and Business stories

The easiest merging action happens when there is a clear association between a PO's Story and a Technical Story. You can then augment the original Business Story description by adding the Technical Story details. Splitting the PO's Stories that are too big can be done using many methods as long as the resulting Stories still make sense for the PO. From time to time, one or more Technical Stories will inspire the PO to create a feature around them. As the team goes over the whole Backlog, new ideas will probably take shape while the importance of other concepts might fade away and could be removed from the

Backlog. Finally, as you may have guessed, method #5 is the the one you want to avoid at all costs. Still, expect that you will have some Technical Stories in your Backlog and try your best to limit their number and get rid of them as early as possible.

At any point during this process, if the scope must be modified, it is imperative to keep the stakeholders informed. This can be done using the same method as described in the previous *3.3 Assessment Period* section.

One last check

You have now reached another important point. The vision of the PO has met the reality of the Dev Team and the result is represented in the Backlog as a single list of stories, epics or technical stories. This is a good moment to take a step back and and ask yourself these questions (from the point of view of both vision and technology):

Does this list really represent the project?
Are we missing something important?
Does this list respect the budget and expertise in place?
If we build all of this, will we achieve the objectives?

If things are missing, add them to the list until you feel it represents the project. Think of it as a rough sketch that is covering all the important parts but is not so detailed that it becomes a burden to create. Like a rough drawing, if you squint your eyes you can appreciate the whole picture and imagine the small details that will later appear.

5.3 Step 2: CrumbScale Points Distribution

The content of the whole Backlog is fresh in the mind of the Scrum Team and we want to move right along with the effort points distribution before this information gets old. Point distribution will be done in two deceivingly simple steps designed to prevent our brain from getting in our way. Tool-wise, it is a good time to get a spreadsheet ready containing the full list of Stories. Minimally, this spreadsheet should have the three following columns: Story Name, Description, Effort Points. To maximize the screen real estate, those three columns should be the only visible columns, taking the full width of the screen. Again, to maximize the number of lines visible, it is recommended to set your spreadsheet in full view mode, hide the taskbar and collapse the toolbar/ribbon. I want more pixels, I say! More pixels!

It is also important not to use completed Stories while doing the CrumbScale estimation. The list to be estimated should therefore **only be using new Stories** that have not been worked on by the Dev Team. This important prerequisite will prevent corrupting the Point Scale and the resulting estimation tool. This is meant to avoid cognitive biases preventing us from estimating the effort of a future task the same way we estimate completed tasks. More information on this can be found in the Annex (*8 ANNEX - How CrumbScale Works*).

The next two steps of the CrumbScale estimation are meant to be done at blistering speed, estimating 30 to 60 Stories per hour. Our goal here is to only get the relative size of all the Backlog elements. The steps are simple and so should the discussions be between the Scrum Team members.

Remember the two following tips to speed up the estimation process:

1. Ideally, the Dev Team should have participated in the Stories creation process and thus already understand the intent behind each item of the Backlog. This basic understanding will speed up the discussions while avoiding the need to explain the context of each Story. Minimally, the Dev Team members who did not participate in the Stories creation should have the whole Backlog presented to them before the estimation activity.

2. Only detail the Stories enough to estimate the effort. Any extra information will only slow you down. During the estimation activity the goal is not to get the stories ready for a sprint planning.

Size Ordering

By only asking ourselves the simple question "It this Story bigger than that other one?", we will take the Backlog elements, one-by-one, and drop them into an ordered list until all the items are transferred from the initial *unordered* list into the new *ordered* list. This new list will be ordered by effort size where the size is not based on the elapsed time but on the amount of work (effort) needed, whether this amount results from quantity or from complexity. For example a very simple but repetitive task may be the same *effort size* as a single but complex task (e.g. the creation a single complex algorithm might take as much effort as a repetitive refactoring job). A final preparation to help you in this comparison process is to have your *Definition of Done* at hand. Before starting, your spreadsheet should look like the following Figure 5.5, where the unordered list is at the bottom, leaving space at the top to create the ordered list.

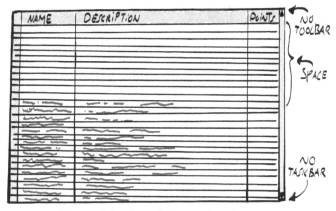

Figure 5.5 – Spreadsheet Before Ordering

Now that we are ready to start, we will take the elements from the unordered bottom list, one-by-one and drop them into the top list while sorting them by size. As you may have guessed, there are a few rules for this to work properly. The top (ordered) list will be ordered from big to small from the top to the bottom (big stories at the top, smaller ones at the bottom. See the following Figure 5.6). 1) Take a new Story from the Unordered list and insert it into the Ordered list by entering from the bottom, going up. 2) As you are moving up in the Ordered list, for each Story you encounter ask the question "Is this new Story bigger than that other one?" If the answer is *yes*, move the Story up by one position and ask the question again. Repeat until you have either found a Story that is bigger or reached the top of the list. 3) Once the answer is *no* (or you have reached the top), you have found the right spot to drop the Story. This process should never take more than 2-4 minutes per Story.

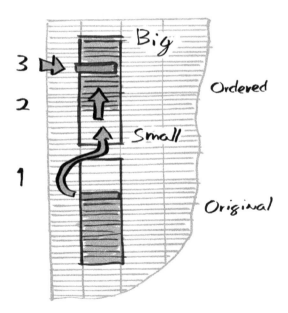

Figure 5.6 – Moving items from the unordered list into the ordered list

Take the next Story in the bottom list and repeat the process until all the Unordered Stories are inserted into the Ordered list. Each new Story is inserted this way, from the bottom up, from the smallest to the biggest, and the size comparison <u>must</u> be done for each Story encountered. This will create a smooth graduation of ever increasing effort size. This smooth graduation is an essential part of the CrumbScale method. Yet, even if this first step sounds simple, everybody makes the same mistake. After a while, the second list will begin to grow and you will be tempted start dropping things directly into the list instead of inserting them from the bottom and moving up one Story at a time. This is a sure way to create errors in the sorting. Our brains are easily tricked and this method, even if it feels babyish, is designed to keep us from making mistakes. Here is another important point: as you insert the items into the top list, you will sometimes find an ordering mistake. Most mistakes are created by not follow the previous rule but honest mistakes will also happen. You must keep the size progression smooth. The bottom of the ordered list is populated by the tiny elements with the smaller size differences and therefore a miscalculation can easily happen. Fix it right away. Remember that you are only doing this process once for the whole project.

On a side note: the software developers amongst you already recognize this procedure as a form of Insertion Sort[26] algorithm. Simple but effective, it is easy for anybody to understand the rules but it can get boring so stay focused and be the best sorters you can be. This way of sorting stories can also be compared to the Relative Mass Valuation[27] method, but CrumbScale will result in a smoother graduation of all the stories instead of having a stepped scale comprised of a few large groups of elements.

---

[26] Press et al. (1992). Numerical Recipes in C. Cambridge, New York, Melbourne: Cambridge University Press, pp.330-331
[27] Green. D. (2014). *3 Powerful Estimation Techniques for Scrum Teams*. [Online] Available at: https://www.sitepoint.com/3-powerful-estimation-techniques-for-agile-teams/ [Accessed 25 Fev. 2017]

Troubleshooting - ordering step

I don't know which Story to pick first
- When picking Stories from the unordered list, simply pick the top one. It is actually preferable for the unordered list to be randomly shuffled, keeping us from the temptation to insert more than one Story at a time or automatically dropping a new Story next to the last inserted Story.

Not sure where to insert a Story
- Look 4-5 positions down for something clearly smaller and come back up or look 4-5 positions up for something clearly bigger and come down from there. In a sense, finding a clear upper and lower bound and working your way toward the middle.
- Try to find more specific reasons why a Story is bigger or smaller than another like: this Story doesn't involve the database; this Story touches a part of the system which we are less familiar with; this Story triggers a series of code refactoring.

Some stories are unclear
- With the help of the PO and the Dev Team expertise, try to clarify the Story or tweak the features description to find an agreeable scenario. We assume (and highly recommend) the Dev Team has participated in the Stories creation process and already understands the intent behind each item of the Backlog. Without this, it will take a long time to explain each Story from scratch.
- Estimate using the worst case scenario. This will likely result in an Epic (large Story) that will need to be split when the time comes during the Production Period.
- If the Story is part of the MVP or a major risk, you should right away create a Spike[28] Story to clarify the situation. This Spike must be clear and easy to estimate.
- If a Story is taking too long to estimate, put it aside and come back to it once you are done with the rest.

---

[28] ExtremeProgramming. *Create a Spike Solution*. [Online] Available at http://www.extremeprogramming.org/rules/spike.html [Accessed 28 Feb. 2017]

It's taking too much time

- This step should take less than 4 minutes per Story even for first time users. We assume (and highly recommend) the Dev Team has participated in the Stories creation process and already understands the intent behind each item of the Backlog. Without this, it will take a long time to explain each Story from scratch.
- You are maybe sharing too much information. As you go up the list, for each Story, you only need enough information to answer the question "Is this new Story bigger than that other one?" Getting in too much detail will only slow the process.
- Maybe the team doesn't have enough expertise to estimate this Backlog. An expert collaborator might be needed to help estimate it and, later on, support them during actual development.

The scale is not smooth

- You may not have enough Stories (i.e. less than 40). In this non-optimal case, it is likely that your scale is not smooth. Even though it is usable, it is recommended to bonify the scale with more Stories as new ones appear during the Production Period. Once you have 40-60 Stories in your scale, it should be smooth and you can stop adding stories to it.
- Stories were probably not inserted in the list by the very bottom and moved up by asking the question "Is this bigger than that?" Find the misplaced Stories and re-insert them the proper way.

Points Distribution

This second half of the CrumbScale points distribution goes much faster than the first one. Working with our newly created ordered list, we will distribute the effort points starting at the bottom of the list and moving up. We will use the following measuring scale:

½, 1, 2, 3, 5, 8, 13, 20, 40, 100

Figure 5.7 – CrumbScale measure scale

At the bottom of the ordered Stories list you will almost certainly have really small tasks falling in the easy work category. If you had to include such a task in your work day, it would have no impact on your schedule. I always call such *easy* work "crumbs" hence the name of the method. Crumbs are the small things that must be done but are so small that it is annoying to even list them. Examples of crumbs are: installing a software, configuring a system or gathering some test data. Give the value of ½ to every crumb as you go up the list until you find the first Story that doesn't fit the 'crumbs' definition. This Story is the first sizable Story and you can give it the value of 1.

As you now go up the list, ask the question "Is this next Story the same size or [almost] twice as big as the last Story?". If this next Story is clearly bigger (almost twice the size), switch to the next value of our CrumbScale measure and keep going. In other words, if you were currently assigning values of 1, you switch to the next value of 2. If you were currently assigning values of 2, you switch to the next value of 3*. Keep assigning values and incrementing to the next level of the scale when needed until you have reached the top of the list. This process should never take more than 1-2 minutes per Story.

The step between 2 and 3, being only an increase of 50%, is smaller than the other. Because we are working at macro level estimation and for the sake of simplicity, we will still ask the same question when passing from 2 to 3; "Is this next Story the same size or [almost] twice as big as the last Story?"

Once you are scoring stories with 20 or more you are now in the epics. If some of those stories are essential for the project, they will most likely have to be broken down into smaller stories. As you finish assigning points to all your stories, most of the stories (around 70-80%) should have values ranging from 1 to 13 (i.e. smaller than epics).

And this is it, you have a full CrumbScale Backlog estimated in effort points. The only skill needed was knowing if one task was bigger than another.

Troubleshooting - effort distribution step

Mostly small stories of 3 points or less
- This indicates a lack of complexity and unknowns in the project. Even though it is OK to continue using Scrum, a large set of known work is better managed through a Kanban process.

MVP Stories are in the Epic range (20 or more)
- Those Epics must be split and estimated using the CrumbScale estimation tool.

Mostly large stories of 8 points or more
- The Dev Team may have underdeveloped skills for Story creation and Story splitting.
- By overestimating the small work, the team may have incremented too quickly through the lower part of the scale (i.e. through 1, 2, 3, 5 and 8). If this is the case, redoing the points estimation exercise should fix the problem. Start back with the crumbs and work your way up, hopefully at a slower pace.

- Maybe the team doesn't have enough expertise to estimate this Backlog. An expert collaborator might be needed to help estimate it and later on during actual development.
- This may simply be an enormous project and it would be better to split more of the important or riskier Stories. This will help with planning and predictability.

Some values underrepresented or not present in the scale

- Later on in the project, as you use the CrumbScale tool, if you find new Stories that could represent those underrepresented values, take the time to complete the scale until the values 1 to 13 are represented by 4-5 Stories each.

It's taking too much time

- This process is normally much faster than step 1 (ordering by size) and should take less than 2 minutes per Story even for first time users. Same as in Step 1, we assume (and highly recommend) the Dev Team has participated in the Stories creation process and already understands the intent behind each item of the Backlog. Without this, it will take a long time to explain each Story from scratch.
- You are maybe sharing too much information. As you go up the list, for each Story, you only need enough information to answer the question "Is this next Story the same size or [almost] twice as big as the last Story?" Getting in too much detail will only slow the process.
- Maybe the team doesn't have enough expertise to estimate this Backlog. An expert collaborator might be needed to help estimate it and later on during actual development.

CrumbScale Estimation Tool

Not only have you estimated all your stories rapidly, an important artifact has also been created. The CrumbScale estimation tool. The ordered list with the added effort points, is now your master reference scale which will help you rapidly estimate any new items that will inevitably appear as the project progresses.

*Important note: Once you have created your estimation tool, **it will not change** for the rest of the project. Those original estimates must remain as they act as an anchor to prevent your future estimations to drift as your skills are evolving.*

It gives you the superpower of estimating new stories under 30 seconds. It is then important to keep a copy of this tool. A good practice is to keep 2-3 printed copies in the Dev Team area so it can be brought out rapidly if an estimation is needed. Let's see how this works.

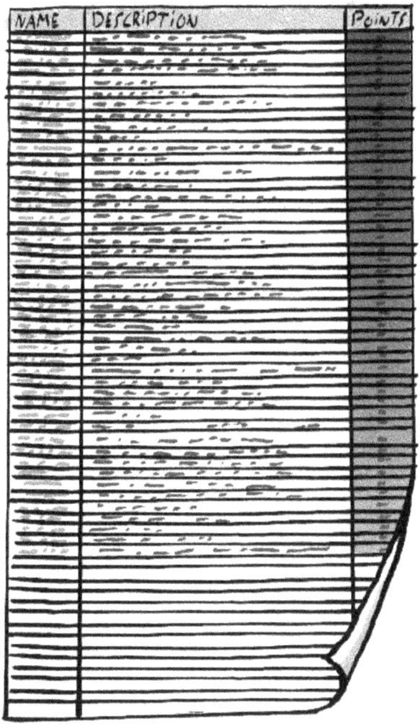

Figure 5.8 – CrumbScale estimation tool

As an example, imagine you are in an ongoing project. This is Sprint-5 and something big has happened forcing the PO to tweak the vision. The PO has created a new Story for the Backlog and he presents it to at least 2 of the core developers that were present at the creation of the Backlog. They listen to the PO's presentation, ask a few questions and agree on the high level technology needed to produce this Story. They then turn around, find the closest CrumbScale estimation tool and, starting from the bottom of the scale, move the new Story up the scale trying to find similar work in the list. Within seconds, they will find an area in the scale where this new Story would fit. They then look at the points in this area, find that there is a bunch of stories with the value of 5 and give this new Story the value of 5. Voila! *The 30 seconds estimation*[29] is now reality. Now, you can put this Story in your Backlog and confidently give it an effort value of 5 points.

A Story estimated with CrumbScale is not inserted in the CrumbScale estimation tool (which would modify the tool), it simply gets an effort point value. Using the tool does not modify it as it must remain the same for the whole project.

I know, some of you are on your knees right now, crying "Why?" and wondering where was this method during all your years of development. It's all good. You are now a points estimation superhero and can use these powers for the greater good. But, no capes!

Troubleshooting - CrumbScale Estimation Tool

The scale has less than 40 items
- Later on in the project, as you use the CrumbScale tool, if you find new Stories that could represent the underrepresented values, take the time to bonify the scale until the values 1 to 13 are represented by 4-5 Stories each.

---

[29] I often call the CrumbScale estimation tool; *The 30 seconds estimation tool.*

The new Story falls exactly in between two scale values

- If, for example, the new Story falls between the values 3 and 5, ask the two following questions; "Is this new Story the same size or [almost] twice as big as the 3 points Story?" and "Is this new Story the same size or [almost] twice as small as the 5 points Story?"

Estimating with the scale takes longer than 30-60 seconds

- Focus only on finding similar work in the list. Do not go into details.
- Don't try to find an exact place in the scale for the new Story. If a zone of 4 or 5 Stories looks about right and they all have the same effort value (e.g. they all have a value of 5), simply assign that effort value to the new Story.
- A Story of a new type may not be comparable with the content of the CrumbScale tool (e.g. new technology, new type of work, new expertise, ...). Somebody on the Scrum Team who is familiar with the content of the CrumbScale tool and knows this new type of work must do the points estimation. Similar to the process used to distribute the initial effort points, insert this new Story from the bottom of the list and move up the list by asking "It this new Story bigger than that other one?" until you find the right position and thus the right effort points given by the neighbouring Stories. It would be a good practice to represent this new type of work in the CrumbScale by modifying the tool as new Stories of this type are created.
- A big change in technology or vision may create a new set of Stories for which the current CrumbScale tool makes no sense. In this extreme case, you may be forced to create a new CrumbScale tool using the new batch of stories.

Expert trick for large Backlogs

Note: First time users must be able to estimate 20-30 stories per hour while CrumbScale experts will be able to estimate upwards of 80 stories per hour. CrumbScale was developed to support Backlogs of 400+ stories which were estimated in half a day using this method.

Expert trick: If you have a large Backlog of (e.g. 150 or more stories), it is possible to make the CrumbScale tool using only 40-60 stories and then use the resulting tool to rapidly estimate the rest of The Backlog. This is a little more risky since great care must be taken when selecting the 40-60 stories which will create your tool. Those stories must, as much as humanly possible, represent the Backlog as a whole. To do so, this sub-selection should contain small, medium and large stories and cover all types of developments, technologies and risks. Teams using this approach can estimate in the upward of 100+ stories per hour.

5.4 Step 3: Prioritization, Scoping and Planning

We are now almost ready to start Sprint-1. All we need is an initial PO prioritization, the Dev Team's first sprint planning and a bit of release planning and scoping. To do all this we will need the following basic information:

- The Backlog containing minimally the MVP
- A MoSCoW prioritization of the Stories
- Effort points for those items
- A prioritization of the Stories by business value
- The initial effort velocity of the team (from Sprint-1 planning)
- The sprint lengths (in weeks)
- The cut off date (when there is no more time or no more money)

If your project has followed the steps in this book, you already have the Backlog estimated in effort points. To move forward in our commentary, we will use data from a fictitious project. Let's call it ProjectX.

Here is what we know about ProjectX so far:

- All items are estimated in points
  - The Backlog total is 684
- The length of the sprints will be 2 weeks
- The cut off date is coming up in 18 weeks

From only this we can already derive other Agile information. First, with the cut off date and the sprint length we know the project can not be longer than 9 sprints. Combining this information with the total of points, tells us that the team would need an effort velocity of 76 points in order to deliver the whole Backlog within the given time. Often, when the senior developers are looking at the content of the Backlog and this ideal effort velocity, they will be able to detect if it is in the realm of the possible.

> *Putting numbers aside for a second, it is now a good time for transferring the list of Stories from its current spreadsheet form into the Agile/Scrum software of your choice.*

To continue planning we will need more information and the PO can get things started by separating the MVP from the rest of the work. For that, I prefer using the MoSCoW prioritization technique. The *Must*, *Should* and *Could* can define anything you want, but for me the *Must* is the bare minimum, the passing grade of 60% or, in other words, the MVP. The *Should* defines the necessary functionalities to complete the project and achieve 100% of the target business value. Finally, the *Could* is the special touch that would make the project unique and innovative, separating it from the competition. To keep things simple in ProjectX, we will only use the *Must* as the MVP and regard the rest as optional.

But what about the *Won't*? Any work that has a remote chance of being released in the project should minimally be a *Could*. Because we want to concentrate our precious Backlog maintenance time for the important things, the *Won't* are simply a distraction we can't afford. On the other hand, if you are a data maniac, a hoarder or a squirrel, you can stash the *Won't* away, as long as they are not visible in the Backlog.

Once the PO has identified the MoSCoW, the next step is to regroup all the *Must* Stories at the top of the Backlog, followed by the *Should* and, finally the *Could* at the bottom. The PO can then prioritize the Stories within each sub-group of MoSCoW. The result should look something like the following Figure 5.9.

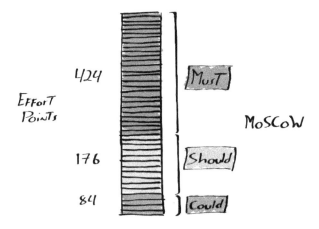

Figure 5.9 – MoSCoW Levels and Effort Points

Because we have effort points on all of the Stories, we now know the total of points for each level of the MoSCoW. For ProjectX, the *Must* total is 424, the *Should* total is 176 and the *Could* total is 84. Armed with this new information, we calculate that a velocity of 47 is needed to deliver the Must (MVP) stories in 9 sprints. This gives us our worst case scenario while a velocity of 76 (delivering the whole Backlog) is our optimistic scenario. The middle ground here would be a velocity of 61.5

points which would give us wiggle room to deliver the MVP while delivering some of the quality Stories. Calculating a "middle ground" velocity this way is one way of adding a buffer to ensure the MVP. It also has the advantage of being proportional to the size of the *Should* and *Could* Stories. Not very scientific but a good starting point.

Another way to ensure the delivery of the MVP while minimizing the buffer, starts by identifying the last *Must* and projecting in which sprint it will fall. Finding the last *Must* is easy since we have the MoSCoW information and a prioritized Backlog. The *Last Must* Story is at the bottom of the *Must* group. Of course, in another project you may want to ensure the delivery of the *Must* and the *Should* and, in such a case, you would want to identify the last *Should*. For ProjectX, we will ensure the delivery of the MVP by identifying the last *Must*.

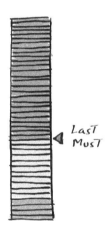

Figure 5.10 – Last Must Story needed for the MVP release

To continue planning we will need to project the sprint into the Backlog which is only possible if we have the effort velocity of the Dev Team. Sadly, this value will only be stable after 2-3 sprints so we will need to use something else. The next best thing is to use the forecasted number of points from sprint planning #1 with a good margin of error.

Sprint planning 1

A little note on sprint planning: it is always good for the PO to start this event by explaining the logic behind his priorities and show how the technology's reality was respected in the process. Personally, I also use this moment to ensure the comprehension of all the Dev Team members by randomly pointing at items in the Backlog and asking a person to describe it. If all the previous steps were done properly, every Scrum Team member should be able to either explain any given Story or, minimally, understand who in the team can explain that Story. I often do the sprint planning #1 a few days before the start of Sprint-1. This is helpful at many levels as it provides the PO with the first predicted effort velocity, gives him time to do some initial planning and leaves time to tweak the Stories if a scoping is required.

OK, I will address the elephant in the room. I know many of you just passed out when I mentioned that we could use the Sprint-1 planned velocity for planning. How can that be a meaningful value? Yes, this value is probably off by a good margin, but it is still the best prediction around. Disregarding external influences and focusing on the team, here are the main factors to gauge the margin of error of this initial effort prediction:

- How long this Dev Team has been working together
- Seniority of the Dev Team
- Team expertise
- Number of risks and unknowns in the Backlog

I was lucky enough to have seen projects where the team knew each other by heart and had the right expertise for the project. In these conditions, I was able to trust the initial velocity within +-30%. Still, when using this initial forecasted velocity, I wait until sprint 2 or 3 before feeling confident about planning. Even with a large margin of error, I always find it more performant to start planning at Sprint-1 and tweak as the velocity is stabilizing. I also feel compelled to plan this way because I don't trust release prediction methods that are not linked to the team's effort velocity. When done this way, predictability becomes a team effort where the PO, by keeping the Backlog relevant and by being available, will support the Dev Team's sprint commitment. At the same time, the Development Team, by estimating the Backlog effort and by stabilizing their effort velocity, will help the PO to plan and deliver the committed features.

For our ProjectX example, we will say that the Dev Team had a sprint planning #1 resulting in a forecasted effort velocity of 45 points.

Release Planning And Scoping

Here is what we know about ProjectX so far:

- All items are estimated in points
  - The Backlog total is 684
  - Must total is 424
  - Should total is 176
  - Could total is 84
- The length of the sprints will be 2 weeks
- The cut off date is coming up in 18 weeks
- The project will have 9 sprints
- The required velocities are:
  - 47 for the *Must*
  - 67 if we include the *Should*
  - 76 if we also include the *Could*
- Sprint-1 planning predicts the Dev Team velocity at 45 points

Knowing the forecasted velocity of 45, in order to deliver the whole Backlog, we would require to nearly double this velocity. Betting on a 70% velocity increase is suicidal. On the other hand, delivering the *Must* is clearly within reach. Since ProjectX aims minimally to ensure the MVP, let's plan around the *Must* only.

Now we need a buffer and, depending on the circumstances, you can either leave 15% after the last *Must* item or use the last sprint all together as a buffer. For projectX, let's see what would happen if we chose to use the last sprint as our buffer. This would bring down the total of sprints to 8 instead of 9. It may look big but let's calculate the real impact of creating this 1-sprint buffer. The 424 points of the *Must* in 8 sprints would demand a velocity of 53 or a 17% increase of the forecasted speed of 45. This we can live with. We now project sprints of 53 points into the Backlog to see what it would look like.

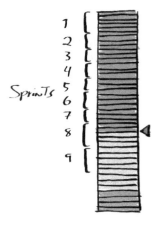

Figure 5.11 – Sprint projection based on velocity

Because we took the time to calculate a velocity aiming at giving us a one sprint buffer, it is no surprise to see the Last Must sitting nicely within sprint 8. In this scenario, there is even some 'wiggle room' which will enable the PO to safely prioritize all the Musts and play with different outcomes. On the other hand the entire scope doesn't fit in the allotted time and the PO can already give a heads up to the stakeholders.

Of course ProjectX is not a difficult situation. Since many things can go wrong in real projects, here are three scary, yet realistic, scenarios. Don't worry, I have lived through and survived them all. Akin to the ProjectX example, the following three scenarios are all aiming at securing the delivery of the MVP.

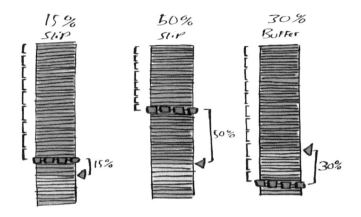

Figure 5.12 – Difficult sprints projection examples

The 15% slip scenario can be easily corrected if the vision is flexible. In fact when your initial planning falls within 15-20% of the goal, you are in good shape. If you deliver enough projects using CrumbScale, such a situation is your normal bread and butter and you should feel pretty confident about shipping the MVP with room to spare. As the PO, after this kind of initial planning, I would go back over the *Must* stories and look for easy compromises in each one. I will also take a long look at the stories where the effort is spent on gambling with unknowns. Depending on the situation, it can be easier to remove one big unknown instead of impacting many stories.

The 50% slip scenario is not good and could be on the frontier of catastrophe, yet, let's see what we can do. I have personally faced this challenged several times and, unless your *Musts* are already riddled with risks or there is no more flexibility in the vision, you should be able to find a solution. Correcting such a slip will need the participation of more than the Scrum Team as we will surely need to also tweak the scope and the budget. To get this project on track, the Scrum Team with the help of the stakeholders and organization, may need to make drastic cuts to the scope, moving the delivery date or staffing more experts and, most of the time, the best solution will be a mix of compromises coming from all sides. For the Team, all those tweaks will generate a slew of new stories to estimate and insert in the Backlog. Luckily, CrumbScale estimation is fast, making it simple to confirm the scope of a new solution.

The final scenario may look perfect but you still must confirm the velocity over the first three sprints. Like the proverb says "Hope for the best but prepare for the worst."[30]. It is still possible that the Dev Team might have underestimated the complexity, especially if the team is junior or does not have a lot of expertise on the riskier elements. On the other hand, once the velocity is confirmed, you can now plan for many positive outcomes. You could commit to delivering the *Shoulds* and even the *Coulds* as if they were *Musts*. You could plan for an early release date. Finally, when thinking at a more organisational level, you could even evaluate the impact of freeing 1 or 2 resources. The goal in this last example would be to slow your effort velocity down without endangering the MVP.

Back to ProjectX. As you have probably noticed in Figure 5.12, we can visualise the cut off date in the Backlog by highlighting the end of the last sprint. Let's call this *the Red Line*. All functionalities required for delivery must fit above this Red Line, including the buffer. In the case of ProjectX, this would be all the *Must* stories plus a buffer. Keep your eyes on the items around this line and make sure the right ones are above it.

[30] Angelou. M. (1969). *I Know Why the Caged Bird Sings*. Random House

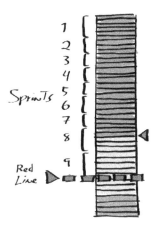

Figure 5.13 – Identify the release deadline as the 'Red Line'

Now that we can see the Last Must and the Red Line, we must create a buffer between them. In what is considered a 'normal' software development project, a 15% to 20% initial buffer is a good practice. Like any normal buffer, it is filled with non-critical items which, ~~if~~ when things start slipping, we can discard some of them to protect the last *Must* from slipping beyond the Red Line.

If you do not have a 15 % buffer, here are a few ways to create one: You can review the least important *Must* stories and consider changing some of them into *Shoulds*. With the help of the Dev Team, you can change the scope of some big stories and re-estimate them down.

Putting it all together, this is what a completed CrumbScale Backlog would look like after the initial prioritization:

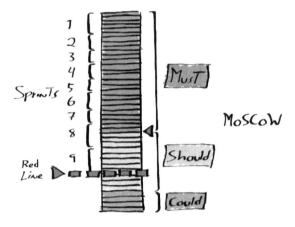

Figure 5.14 – Backlog ready for Sprint-1

After all this work, it is important to let the PO do a final review and prioritization on his own. During this time, he may have questions here and there but he should be able to do most of the work alone while learning to master the Backlog content. This is an important moment for the PO. It builds confidence in the ability to act as the 'pilot' of this Backlog. On top of having the business domain knowledge to maintain, at this point, the PO should also have acquired some understanding of the Dev Team's reality and the technological reality. He should have enough knowledge to make good high level decisions through prioritization of the Backlog.

This last section has covered the very basics of CrumbScale Backlog planning. In real life you may face many challenges that will impact this exercise. While planning at this early stage you may already know about uneven staffing along the project duration, multiple releases, sharing your resource capacity or critical outside dependencies blocking some stories. You can compensate for any and all of those constraints by adapting your planning and keep tweaking it as the project moves forward and your context evolves.

6 Sorting the Unknowns

It was board game night and, while playing Settlers of Catan[31] with friends, I spent an entire game fixing up the crooked game tiles forming the play area. It turned out that every time I was looking away, one of my 'friends' would knock the tiles slightly out of alignment. Apparently, their goal was to see how long it would take before I called foul play. In the end, I spent nearly the whole game fixing misplaced tiles while they were running their experiment. One could say that I like sorting, knolling and aligning things... or one could say I need professional help or even new friends.

Maybe it is the programmer in me or my amateur infatuation with mathematics but I have a tendency to classify things into groups and endlessly refine this classification. For anybody who appreciates sorting and pattern recognition, this is not a chore but a challenge. In my opinion, a less potent form of this disease is *knolling[32]* which, for some crazy reason, I rarely do. When it comes to software development, this classification addiction became handy for separating the risks from the normal development work.

---

[31] Settlers of Catan board game, catan.com, http://www.catan.com/
[32] *"Knolling is the process of arranging related objects in parallel or 90-degree angles [...]"*, Wikipedia, https://en.wikipedia.org/wiki/Knolling

In software development, a skill for rapidly estimating the size and complexity[33] of work is valuable. It is the burden of all software developers to acquire this ability and use it to estimate work at different scales such as tasks, stories and, depending on the career path, epics and whole projects. Acquiring this skill is not straightforward and, sadly, it normally is a trial and error process. Having been through it myself, having seen my peers struggle and countless juniors looking like deers caught in headlights, I can say that any help is welcome to speed up this learning experience.

Around 2006-2008, with some 12 years of development behind me, I felt the need to improve the process of rapid assessment. To get started, I paid more attention in moments when rapid assessment was important and, especially, how it could be more efficient and effective. After a few projects and with trial and error, a method took form and it became a real goto tool for me and my team. I called it the Easy-Normal-Hard (ENH) method and the name has stuck since then. This chapter will explain the basic context in which it was created, how it works and when to use it.

Note: Even though I use it myself, I did not include my complexity sorting method in the description of the other two methods (Handle it or Hand it Over and CrumbScale) considering, as a stand alone tool, it can be used throughout the whole project, even during the Production Period. I then highly recommend using Easy-Normal-Hard during the Assessment period and the CrumbScale Backlog creation.

6.1 About Managing Complexity

Before we describe the ENH rapid assessment method, I would like share how I picture effort complexity and where it fits in the big picture of a project's life.

---

[33]   By 'complexity' I refer to the technical or technological *project complexity* and not other *dimensions* of risk like resources User, Requirements, Planning, Control, and so on.

The lowest level of effort is the task level where micro estimation is used to calculate the projected development time in hours. This level of estimation is also known as 'precise estimation'. This type of estimation is extremely detailed and time consuming. The second level of effort is the Story/Epic level where macro estimation compares the relative sizes of effort using points which are much faster to estimate. Finally, the third and most abstract level of effort is the Features level containing mostly bigger concepts sometimes called functionalities, themes, journeys or even entire projects. In order to keep things simple, I will simply call this level 'Features'. At this level, you often see the use of rough estimation methods like Man Months, T-shirt Size and comparison with reference projects. This level is meant to gauge the feasibility of the project without investing in a lengthy estimation process.

The following table illustrates this so that you can easily see the relation between the effort levels, the Scrum levels, the Effort Dimensions (qualifying the effort) and the Estimation Units.

Project Periods	Effort Levels	Scrum Levels	Effort Dimensions	Estimation Units
Incubation	Features or bigger (Ginormous)	Functionalities or Project	Feasibility	T-Shirt Size, Man Months, etc...
Assessment & Planning	Story and Epics (Macro)	Backlog	Scope	Points
Production	Task (Micro)	Sprint	Time	Hours

Figure 6.1 – Effort Levels

The step between each estimation level is pretty large and, in most cases, there should be minimal overlap between them. Overlaps can occur when a big task is also a small Story or when a large Epic could be an entire feature. In such cases, the item will have the amazing chance of being estimated twice in two different scales. Looking at the last column, we can see the estimation units (and methods) used for each effort level. For each estimation level, from the bottom toward the top, the time invested in estimation should reduce dramatically (minimally by an order of magnitude) at each level otherwise it would be impractical.

To go further in our understanding of complexity in a project, we can create a matrix using the three levels of complexity (easy, normal and hard) and the three levels of effort (Features, Stories and tasks). This creates a grid on which we can plot how complexity progresses through the project as the vision switches from a list of functionalities (features) to a Backlog (stories) and finally into a Sprint Backlog (Tasks). To visualize this, we will plot 4 different regions, one for each type of *implementation risk*[34]: the *Unknowns* with maximum risk, the *Chaos* with standard software development risk, the *Knowns* with low risk, and the *Free* with no risk.

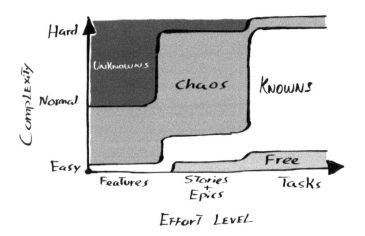

Figure 6.2 – Complexity Progression graph (Standard)

---

[34] Here 'Implementation Risk' defines the complexity of coding a given feature from the point of view of the Development Team.

Looking at this diagram, the progression of complexity should represent how much risk your organization is ready to accept at the Strategic level (when considering a project), the Project level (when confirming the scope in the Product Backlog (Backlog)) and the Tactical level (when producing code). In the Complexity Progression graph, the boundaries between the different types of complexities may vary depending on the type of project and how it regulates the levels of risk it is ready to accept. Here are some of the rules I use for a standard software development project (see Figure 6.2) where you have very little room for experimentation and delivering overrides innovation:

- The Backlog (stories) should contain no more than 15% unknowns or the maximum the Development Team (Dev Team) can handle.
- The sprint (tasks) should not contain unknowns.
- The sprint (tasks) should contain no more than 15-20% of chaos, enabling the team to deliver the sprint increment.

Exploration projects, as a second example, may progress with the following rules and accept some innovation risks. The value in this type of project is centered around learning.

- The Backlog (stories) should contain no more than 40% unknowns.
- The sprint (tasks) should contain no more than 10% unknowns.
- The sprint (tasks) should contain no more than 20-30% of chaos.

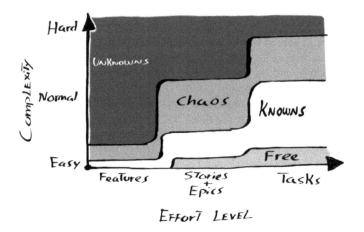

Figure 6.3 – Exploration Complexity Progression

Finally, to show another extreme, we can have a zero-risk project. This scenario can happen when the development work only includes fixes, tweaks and repeats of existing functionalities. This type of development steers clear of chaos and could likely be managed using the Kanban[35] approach instead of Scrum.

- The Backlog (stories) should not contain unknowns.
- The sprint (tasks) should not contain unknowns.
- The sprint (tasks) should contain no more than 10% of chaos.

---

[35] Wikipedia. *Kanban*. [Online] Available athttps://en.wikipedia.org/wiki/Kanban_(development) [Accessed 28 Feb. 2017]

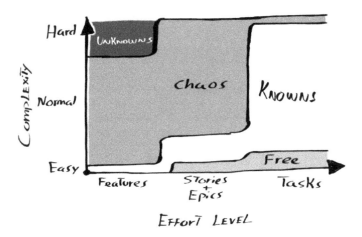

Figure 6.4 – Risk-less Complexity Progression

Things go awry when the Complexity Progression is not aligned with a project's reality. For example, in order to fit more stories into the project planning, a Scrum Team may be forced to take on more unknowns and risk without adjusting the level of acceptable failure rate. Proceeding this way is wishful thinking on the part of the organization and disrespectful to the Scrum Team that suffers unnecessary pressure. On such a path, a project's success and its team's morale will both be at risk. As you move from Features to Stories and from Stories to Tasks, enforce your Complexity Progression by either scoping or staffing accordingly.

6.2 METHOD 3: Easy-Normal-Hard

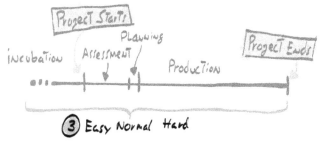

Figure 6.5 – Method 3 in relation to the project timeline

When describing how a physicist will remove the unnecessary details from the problem he is trying to solve, Lawrence Krauss[36] explains the importance of "knowing what to throw out". For a software developer or a Product Owner (PO), it is important not to get tangled in useless time-consuming tasks like a 2 hours management discussion about a 30 minute coding job, or investing countless hours evaluating new risk when you already have no more space for risk. Time spent this way is reducing the amount of functionality and quality put into the project. On top of which, it can open the door for a surplus of risk, jeopardizing the project objectives.

The same way Test Driven Development[37] enables a Dev Team to rapidly and safely code new features, a trusted rapid assessment method enables all the decision makers (PO, Dev Team, experts, leads and managers) to make crucial decisions while saving time.

---

[36] Krauss. L. (2014). *The secret life of physicists*. [Online video] Available at https://www.youtube.com/watch?v=MH4AihOgRBk [Accessed 28 Feb. 2017]

[37] AgileAlliance. *TDD*. [Online] Available at https://www.agilealliance.org/glossary/tdd/ [Accessed 28 Feb. 2017]

When introducing this technique, I often start with the following description:

> "There's three types of tasks: the Easy ones taking no time to do, the Normal ones, which are the standard chaotic work constituting the vast majority of development, and finally, the Hard ones which are high risk unknowns often requiring exploration work to even know if they are doable."

6.2.1 Easy

A good way to detect easy work is by observing the Dev Team when they are talking about it. If they look annoyed simply talking about it, or say "it would be faster to just do it", then you know it's easy work. You may hear this more often from your 'star' developer. You know who I'm talking about, that guy that can make anything happen in a ridiculously short time. If stars have one drawback, it's their estimation discrepancies compared to the team's average. I normally let the experts and the stars identify what is hard while I prefer a majority decision on what is normal and easy.

I often refer to the easy work as 'crumbs' which only applies to tasks and some stories, never to epics and projects. When talking about tasks inside the sprint, easy work encompasses all work that could fit 'on the side' like minor tweaks. Easy work has no impact on your daily schedule. During the sprint planning, such crumbs are normally estimated in seconds. When talking about stories, easy work encompasses the irritatingly small stories which feel more like tasks. With CrumbScale, when an easy Story is estimated in points, it ranks at ½ point and helps define the crumbs of the Backlog. On the other hand, 1 point tasks are not easy. They are one step above the crumbs and are the smallest possible 'Normal' work.

There is rarely risk associated with Easy work. It can often be done alone, by many of the team members, and can be done in many different ways. In the chaos of software development, easy tasks are the outlier sure shots. For the PO, knowing what the team considers *easy* is a big plus. It will influence the prioritization and how far tweaking can be done within a sprint.

What does it mean if much of your work falls in the Easy category? Maybe you are not in the chaos of a normal development project. In such a context a team will get better results by optimizing flow instead of managing chaos. As mentioned previously, your team may find it more efficient to use Kanban instead of Scrum.

6.2.2 Normal

Normal work is the bread and butter of the programmer. It covers all standard types of development like UI, networking, memory management, optimization, and so on. You will find normal work at all levels of the work scale: tasks, Stories, Epics and projects.

Normal work doesn't annoy the programmers like easy work does and it is not flat out scary like the hard work is. When faced with normal work the team will naturally start looking for ways to best attack the problem. It is also the type of work that can be compared with previous experiences or tackled with known methods.

Junior developers and developers lacking the appropriate expertise will often refer to Normal work as being Hard. This is understandable since complexity is relative to the person's skill and knowledge. Like construction workers, programmers are often specialized and cannot simply pick up their coworker's task or perform it as rapidly.

The scope of what is normal for your team will grow with time as they tackle harder and harder problems. Without going into the subject in too much detail, you can hack this growth in many ways and here are two common ways to do that:

You can add specialists or extra senior members to the team, or you can speed up learning through an aggressive innovation management plan by making more space for experimentation.

When defined into stories, normal work will rank (in CrumbScale points) from 1 to 13.

6.2.3 Hard

Very often, hard work will be in the scale of epics or even projects until exploratory work is done to determine its scale or feasibility. Sometimes, hard work will lurk at the frontier it shares with normal work, disguising itself into stories with the same amount of points as other normal Stories. Those are the tricky ones to spot.

When exploded into epics or stories, hard work will rank (in CrumbScale points) from 100 down to 20 and sometimes 13. Hard work will need to be investigated through Spike stories then exploded into stories of average complexity. In a normal development scenario you'll never want to include Hard work into a production sprint as its unknown components will prevent the team from planning it. This classic mistake will almost certainly result in a failure to achieve the sprint goals.

6.3 When to Use This

My definition of Easy, Normal and Hard (ENH) work is purposefully simplistic in order to be instinctively used. Because it is meant as a blazingly fast tool, only practice can help you master it. I will help jumpstart this process by pointing out the crucial moments where this tool is the most effective. Here are my top three scenarios: 1) when building the Backlog and having to limit the risk, 2) when approving new stories added during production and finally, 3) when deciding if an in-sprint 'suggestion' is a harmless tweak or should be pushed to the Backlog as a new Story. All three scenarios are probably well known to you no matter which part you play in a project. Those are important moments where decisions must be taken rapidly while (often) under pressure, and if there is no efficient 'safety net' to filter the risk, your organization will probably either waste time, miss an opportunity or obstruct the project from shipping as planned. In other words, if the safety net you have in place is not efficient, it may take an enormous amount of time to evaluate, identify and control risk. If the safety net is too restrictive, it may prevent more than the risks and restrict innovation. Finally, if the safety net is ineffective or nonexistent, chaos can take over at any time resulting in the failure to achieve predictability and the inability to guarantee any deliveries.

6.3.1 ENH for Backlog

The Backlog creation period is a critical moment where you want to maximize the features by taking just enough risk and still keep a realistic buffer. Sadly this moment in a project is mostly seen as stressful. For the Dev Team, the stress often comes from over-committing on features while risks are being wrongfully downgraded into "normal work" through magical statements like "we'll use a ready made solution for this part" or "we'll find an expert to help us with this". Pressure is a tricky beast. It can make you bend your basic rules and do stupid things. Even after so many years of working in development, I still have to work hard not to get caught up in a Backlog over-commitment. Let's see how I systematically use Easy-Normal-Hard to prevent this.

During the Backlog creation, the principal role of the Easy-Normal-Hard sorting is to help you find the risks and, if needed, start scoping accordingly. A second, but much smaller, advantage of this sorting method is to quickly identify the small work (easy) and put it aside while the bulk of effort is spent on understanding the bigger problems. I consider this a small advantage because the Easy work is normally simple to identify and, no matter what your method is today, you probably already have a good enough way to sniff out the Easy work and not waste time on it.

Scale and Risk are Unique: When estimating, each team, each project and at different points in time, will generate a unique configuration of stories and a unique points estimation scale. If this is a shock, the next one will bum you out. If you ask a team to turn a features list into a Backlog and then ask them to start from scratch and do it again, you will not get the same result. Why? Because doing the task is also a learning experience which will unavoidably affect the results of all future tasks. The same applies to the definition of risk (from a technology implementation point of view). For a given project, at a given time, the definition of risk is unique to each team. What is hard for one team can be easy for another. We can also say that what was hard for a team, as time goes by, can eventually become easy for them. Therefore, a unilateral definition of what is 'Risky' or 'Hard' cannot be imposed on a team and can only be defined by looking at the project through the team's eyes.

Rant

This is why you cannot have some 'senior' programmer defining and estimating work for other people. The resulting breakdown of the work would be meaningless and the estimates... pure poetry. Other than the total inability to ensure a deliverable, this archaic approach is destructive for the team's morale as they are detached from the process while working on 'someone else's list'.

I am not advocating for a chaotic world where each team can turn a project upside-down by taking complete control. A Dev Team is one part in a bigger system and must respect the work of the other contributors. On the other hand, they must have some kind of unique expertise or else why would they even be there? What I advocate for is to let each team design and plan the work that fits within the scope of their expertise. They must do this while respecting the outside constraints coming from other fields of expertise. In such a system, each expert team is fully enabled to apply its expertise and make part of the project their own. Such teams feel empowered.

Separate Normal from Hard: As you are creating the stories for a new Backlog, a trick to know if a Story is 'Hard' is to observe the Dev Team as you describe the Story. If they display signs of distress, it is a Hard Story. This is triggered by the realization that no plan, not even a macro plan, seems to pop in mind for tackling this new Story. After the initial shock, the team will start working out possible solutions and a rough shot-in-the-dark plan should emerge, morphing this monster from an impossibility to a 'maybe'. Clearly you have found Hard work. The worst case scenario is when there is no plan, not even an investigation idea. Then, the Story is most certainly beyond the reach of the team's expertise.

For each feature and Story categorised as Hard, new exploration stories (Spike) should be created to remove the risk and confirm the feasibility. In the Backlog, this is represented by one or more Story-size Spikes of Normal complexity followed by at least one large Epic representing the Hard, and still unknown, feature. Once the exploration work is completed, the Epic can be refined into one or many Stories of Normal complexity.

Limiting Complexity Risk: What is the maximum complexity risk acceptable for a project? Most existing methods of risk management are meant for managers but rarely help the Scrum Team from taking unacceptable levels of risk. This is where Easy-Normal-Hard can help by identifying all the Hard, thus risky, work in each field of expertise. Knowing the real amount of risk and knowing which expertise is impacted can help us protect the project by letting just enough risk into it. Here is how:

We can manage the exact number of risks taken by following yet another simple rule:

In a project, take 1 risk per team plus 1 risk per expert in their respective field.

For example, if I have a Dev Team of 5 developers with 1 network specialist and 1 computer vision specialist, I would only accept 1 network related risk, 1 computer vision related risk and 1 generic team risk. The rest would have to be scoped out. The '1 per expert' rule is self explanatory and simple to apply. Having 1 risk per team is a bit more complicated since it expects that the resolution of the risk to be a team effort. For a mature team this kind of risk is often defined by a large system that will be built through the collaboration of many team members. For a more junior (or inexperienced) team, this kind of risk is sometimes a large task that a senior or expert could have tackled alone but that is still doable through the group effort of juniors or non-experts.

Knowing how much risk the team can take and who would take each of the risks will be important when you will eventually decide on the scope of the project. As you can see, the scope will be tightly linked to the actual team's strengths.

6.3.2 ENH for Added Stories

Because we are not omnipotent, we will uncover major information during the project and, in turn, this will often translate in the creation of new Stories. The trick here is to keep in mind the Standing Orders: *Protect the Team, Protect the Vision and Ship*. In other words, don't let a new Story create unsustainable work, confuse or diminish the vision or put your delivery in danger.

Even if your organization is using Scrum and should maintain a flexible Backlog, you still need to stand guard against the eventual slip-up of over-commitment. Not unlike a recovering alcoholic, we all have it in us to relapse if we get tempted in moments of weakness. There will always be a great opportunity where we 'must' make a custom demo for this conference or add this extra feature that will make all the difference. If something else is pushed aside to make room for those 'last minute opportunities' then everything is OK. On the other hand, they are often simply thrown on top of the pile.

Managing this kind of demand is how the PO protects the team and the project. Still, we live in the real world where people will try to 'tweak' processes, bend the rules or simply impose unconditional decisions. This is when having a PO with a titanium backbone is capital to the project success. Let's look at how, as new stories appear, we can handle them.

When a new Story is considered, the PO can initially decide if it's even worth estimating. This is the first level of protection for the team and the Backlog, and without it the team can become slaves to endless Story estimation. Normally, when acting as a PO, I would approach one or more experts in the Dev Team with the potential new Story and quickly describe it. If it is Easy or Normal work I will add it to the Backlog and mitigate the impact through prioritization and some re-scoping. On the other hand, if it is clearly Hard work for them, I will normally reject this new Story unless, in very rare cases, it is a show stopping Must. Needless to say, I trust my experts implicitly.

Estimation Slaves: Scoping risks by evaluating Hard work and designing possible scenarios should only happen during Proof of concept periods or during the Assessment Period, unless you are doing research or exploration. If you are scoping risks during the Production Period, you are in danger of becoming an estimation slave. A symptom of this affliction manifests itself when new stories are appearing at such a rate that evaluating and estimating them is impacting your sprint velocity.

A Dev Team is not a project simulator. If too many new stories are popping up all the time, your project was probably ill defined at the beginning. Here are the other reasons why this situation happens (based on experience):

- The PO is inventing the project as it goes along in a project where there is no space for experimentation.
- The PO is trying to sneak a new Hard feature into the Backlog by breaking it down into a string of separate Stories with the hope of adding a final task that says "Put it all together to form this monster feature".

- Design is being done reactively and the same Story keeps coming back for estimation in all different shapes and flavours with a note saying "it is not working like I thought it would".

Here of course, I assume that there is only one PO. Sadly, if your organization lets more than one person be in charge of the Backlog, your project is probably doomed. You likely noticed that only the Backlog owner (or whoever controls the Backlog) can turn the team into estimation slaves. This type of situation is less likely to happen if the PO is following the principles in this book and puts the team first.

6.3.3 ENH for Sprint Tweaks

What we call a 'tweak' is an Easy task that can be added on the fly during a sprint with little or no impact on the sprint. Often times when thinking about tweaks, we picture the PO's and stakeholders' demands based on their review of the current work. Tweaks can also come from within the Dev Team as they identify small, non-sprint related or non-critical, technical tasks to improve the code base. Deciding if these on-the-spot demands are harmless tweaks or actual stories to be added to the Backlog can sometimes make or break a sprint.

Normally riding the thin line separating Easy and Normal work, many tweaks will have something in common: a combination of high value and pertinence. It's the perfect moment when the feature is nearly complete, the code is up on the developer's screen and, after pondering on the state of what he just saw, the PO asks, "Can you change the duration of the fade-out?" At this perfect moment, the PO and the developer may rapidly tweak something which, if postponed, would cost much more to do. On the other hand, this demand may be more than a tweak and could nudge the developer on a slippery slope taking him away from his sprint goals. In that case, even though there is a clear value in making the modification, this work is not a tweak and must be clearly described in Story form, estimated and prioritized in the Backlog.

Easy-Normal-Hard can guide you in those critical moments by helping you make fast decisions with confidence. During an ongoing sprint, if a demand is Easy and the developer is confident that he can deliver this extra work while ensuring his sprint goals it is then OK to do it. Anything else should be added to the Backlog as a Story.

It may look radical but it works. It protects the sprint goals, respects the Dev Team and the added Story has a good chance to be completed within the sprint anyway. How can that be? Imagine a modification is quickly dismissed as being 'small' but not Easy. All is not lost. The PO can quickly create a new Story describing this 'small tweak' and prioritize it at the top of the Backlog. Best case scenario (which happens to me often), this small Story will be picked up by someone who completed all of his sprint tasks and is now taking extra work from the top of the Backlog. Worst case scenario, it will fall down in prioritization before the next sprint planning but should still fit in the next sprint, as we often need small stories to top up the Sprint Backlog.

I believe in tweaking features as they are developed in a sprint. The same way bugs discovered during a sprint should be resolved (within the limits of reason) during the same sprint, tweaks should not be pushed forward to form a design debt. While minimizing the accumulation of technical debt is a Dev Team problem, minimizing the accumulation of tweaks into a design debt is a Scrum Team problem. This work is at the frontier of design and implementation and can only be efficient through collaboration.

Working in close relationship between the Dev Team and the stakeholders (including the PO and the client) is an important Agile Value[38] with the potential to speed up development and increase quality.

---

[38] **"Customer collaboration** over contract negotiation", Agilemanifesto.org, http://www.agilemanifesto.org/

As I see it, true collaboration is based on mutual respect and, not unlike a long term relationship, needs constant care to stay healthy. One of the best ways to test and maintain this partnership is by allowing as many in-sprint tweaks as possible without endangering the Sprint Goals. Each time you do, you will learn a little bit more about your team's boundary between Normal and Easy. Each tweak will inform the Dev Team about what is valuable for the PO and the project.

In conclusion, if you are the PO, listen to your experts and trust their opinions. Start your relationship with your experts by giving them 100% of your trust instead of starting from zero and making them 'earn' it. Your experts are humans too and they will have their own doubts to overcome. Your best course of action is to let them know you expect the best but you also understand that we will sometimes fail since you are all taking risks together. With time, they will build their confidence as you get to know them. The PO can make rapid decisions regarding the Backlog items only if he understands the impact of those decisions. The PO will often rely on others to understand the effort impacts or even feasibility. Through a good relationship with the technology experts, he can rapidly assess options, identify one or more b-plans and select a primary solution. When you reach such a symbiosis between the Dev Team and the PO, problem solving becomes a team effort and the resulting solutions are the team's property from which stems full engagement.

7 Conclusion

What are the key elements of a successful development project? What makes a team happy? How can we protect a good idea throughout a project? I tend to ask those questions a lot and, depending on whom I ask and when I ask, answers vary wildly. Sifting through all those realities I see a common trend where engaged people want their endeavours to be meaningful, successful and fun.

Using Scrum, protecting the people on the project, protecting the product vision and, as a group, always figuring out a way to ship the best solution possible, this was the context in which Rally-Point Backlog took shape.

When using those methods, our end goal as a team was not only at the conclusion of the project, but at the end of every project period, every deliverable, every sprint and every meeting. As a team, it always felt like winning as we were crossing the finish line of each step no matter how small. We knew that the job was done and that we could transition and switch 100% of our focus on the next goal.

These are our small wins but most importantly, adding the Rally-Point Backlog layer on top of Scrum enabled us to do the following:

- Engage the Development Team into the project vision and also gain better alignment between the business and technology needs.
- Create a solid points effort estimation to support Agile planning, rapidly gain* predictability and remain* predictable.
- Manage the level of risk accepted into the Backlog throughout the project lifecycle.
- Establish a better collaboration loop between the stakeholders, the Product Owner (PO) and the Development Team (Dev Team).

The gain and maintenance of predictability will happen during the Production Period which, if we are lucky, will be covered in a following book (Rally-Point Backlog / Sprint Dynamics). The initial estimation of the Backlog and the creation of the rapid estimation tool is, on the other hand, covered in this book. ... shameless plug, I know.

Because many methods and project management approaches have a hard time merging the vision and the Dev Team's reality, we often think of the stakeholders' requirements as being in opposition to the technology capabilities. One always being derailed by limitation, and the other never really used to its full potential. Using the Rally-Point Backlog methods will steer you toward true collaboration between the Dev Team, the PO and the stakeholders. The resulting flexibility and alignment for the project were game changing for all the teams I had a chance to work with and I wish this book will help you get the same results.

I hope you have safe, predictable and successful projects.

8 ANNEX - How CrumbScale Works

"The drive toward bigger and better created its own logic."[39]

- Michael Hiltzik

Once you have a good idea for a software development project, two questions must be answered before we can consider giving it the green light; "Can it be done?" and "How much will it cost?" Those two questions come in many forms but will always cover the subjects of feasibility and a quantification of effort and time. To answer the first question, you will either need the right expertise or some experimentation. The second question will entail a form of estimation of the work effort. Then, as soon as the project is launched, somebody (if not everybody), will want to know if it is on track and will deliver on-time and on-budget. To answer this, you will need a way to measure the current rate at which features are completed and compare it to the remaining work. So, in a development project, effort estimation is key unless you are paying with your own money and leading people which are comfortable with no progress measurement. This is a big reason why CrumbScale exists and continues to be improved upon.

Effort estimation took a big leap forward when relative size estimations became popular at the end of the 1990s, starting with the eXtreme Programing "Load factor"[40] which lead to the

---

[39] Hiltzik. M. (2015). *Big Science*. New York, London, Toronto, Sydney, New Delhi: Simon & Schuster, pp.7.

Story Points in the early 2000s. Scrum teams using this method were able to estimate faster and, when done right, did not have to re-estimate as the project progressed. Well, at least this was the promise of using Story Points but, with uneven results and overall confusion on how it works, today it still has a bad reputation outside Scrum circles and sometimes even in Scrum circles. I, myself, after having switched to Scrum in 2005, avoided using points for my first Scrum project while trying to wrap my head around it.

Still, lured by the advantage of faster estimation and the possibility of avoiding re-estimation, I was ready to try points in 2006, but, for it to work, I felt compelled to improve on the existing methods by removing the confusing parts. Initially, it was not supposed to go any further and it could have turned out as a simple twist on the existing Planning Poker method. As said by Michael Hiltzik when explaining how large science projects can snowball under their own power, "The drive toward bigger and better created its own logic." So it was, trying to remove confusion in Story Points triggered other improvements and, bit by bit, transformed the whole thing into a 10 year quest for a simpler, faster and more precise estimation method. CrumbScale.

8.1 Removing Confusion from Points Estimation

The standard Story Points definition states that there is no relation between points and hours[41] but popular methods are confusing users on this particular subject. If you take part in a traditional Wall Session or Planning Poker, you can count in

[40] Beck. K. (2000). *Extreme Programming Explained*. Boston, San Francisco, New York, Toronto, Montreal, London, Munich, Paris, Madrid, Capetown, Sidney, Tokyo, Singapore, Mexico City: Addison-Wesley, pp.178

[41] AgileFAQ. *What is a Story Points?*
https://agilefaq.wordpress.com/2007/11/13/what-is-a-story-point/

seconds the time it takes for one of the participants to ask "How much is one point worth?" or "Do we need a reference before we start estimating?" Humoring these questions will establish the infamous points-hours relationship which is exactly what we are trying to avoid.

CrumbScale avoids these problems altogether by assigning effort points to Stories in a completely different way. Instead of estimating each Story one at a time, CrumbScale will **distribute** the effort points with a two steps process involving all of the Stories. This two steps process (described in section *5.3 Step 2: CrumbScale Points Distribution*) does not need reference Stories to initiate the "estimation" process and thus gets rid of this major point of friction. Also, once the initial CrumbScale point distribution is done, one of the byproducts is the creation of a rapid **estimation** tool. This tool becomes the single reference for all future estimations, further avoiding the creation of a link between points and hours.

Without this "hours vs points" cloud over our heads, here is how I present points to first time users:

- Points are used as a measure of effort for macro estimation in the Backlog while hours can be used for precise estimation at the task level (i.e. in the Sprint Backlog).
- Points represent the relative size of effort quantity, complexity or risk.
- Hours estimation is a precise measurement and points estimation is a relative measurement.
- There should be no relationship between points and hours.
- By stabilizing the amount of points a team commits to and delivers each sprint, we can achieve predictability.
- Points are only meaningful for a given Dev Team in a given Backlog and cannot be compared with other Dev Teams.

Still using the modified Fibonacci series

CrumbScale remains a relative measurement method and benefits from restricting the size selection in the same way Planning Poker does. Because of that, and not wanting to reinvent the wheel, CrumbScale size selection follows in the Planning Poker footsteps which is based on the Fibonacci series[42]:

$$0, 1, 1, 2, 3, 5, 8, 13, 21, 34, 55, 89, 144, 233, 377, 610, 987, 1597, \ldots$$

In this series, each number is the total of the two preceding numbers. As you can see in this scale, if you take away the first 2 elements, we could almost say that the numbers are almost doubling at each step. In reality, the actual ratio between each number averages around 1.62 which is the Golden Ratio[43]. In order to keep things simple, let's agree that this is almost 2 (e.g. the double). Jumping by [almost] two between each value is very practical when judging the relative scale of two things. While small differences are hard for us to judge accurately, most people are pretty good at recognizing if something is either equal or double the size when compared with something else.

When James Grenning invented the Planning Poker[44] method, he initially created a selection of numbers where the estimation precision decreases as the numbers are going up. This was done by increasing the step between the numbers.

$$1, 2, 3, 5, 7, 10, \infty$$

[42] Wikipedia. *Fibonacci number*. [Online] Available at: https://en.wikipedia.org/wiki/Fibonacci_number [Accessed 28 Jan. 2017].
[43] Wikipedia. *Golden ratio.* [Online] Available at: https://en.wikipedia.org/wiki/Golden_ratio [Accessed 28 Jan. 2017].
[44] Grenning. J. (2002). *Planning Poker or How to avoid analysis paralysis while release planning.* [Online] Available at: https://wingman-sw.com/papers/PlanningPoker-v1.1.pdf [Accessed 28 Jan. 2017].

This similarity with the Fibonacci series was clear enough to influence an evolution of the scale into the current popular form:

$$0, \tfrac{1}{2}, 1, 2, 3, 5, 8, 13, 20, 40, \infty, ?$$

In this scale, the '?' represents the impossibility to evaluate the effort. This could be because of a lack of expertise or lack of information. Also, many Planning Poker scales initially included the value '100' but this number is now dropped by many Planning Poker card decks. With CrumbScale we will not need the '0', the '∞' or the '?' but we will keep the '100' which gives us the following scale, as presented earlier in Figure 5.7 :

$$\tfrac{1}{2}, 1, 2, 3, 5, 8, 13, 20, 40, 100$$

As a side note, I have experimented with other scales like powers of 2 (1, 2, 4, 8, 16, 32, ...) but , so far, results were never as good as using the modified Fibonacci scale which has more values in the low range (0.5 to 13) before sharply increasing into the Epics range (20 to 100). This gives a lot of room for the estimation of Normal[45] work and clearly separates it from the Hard or undefined work.

No More Distant Comparisons

When estimating in traditional points methods, we are often faced with what I call distant comparison. This happens when comparing two Stories that are separated by more than one step in the measure scale. This will happen more often at the beginning of the points estimation session where the newer Stories are not necessarily in the same range as the Stories estimated so far (e.g. you only have Stories ranging from 1 to 8

---

[45] As defined in the Easy-Normal-Hard method.

and you are now estimating a Story at 20 points). This is problematic since the further you get from a known reference point the less precise your points estimation will be. Using CrumbScale solves this issue by relying only on the estimation of items of same size, one size up or one size down. This is done by asking only two questions "Is this bigger than that?" and "Is this the same size or double the size of that?". By removing distant comparison, CrumbScale improves the precision of points estimation while removing confusion and long debates.

8.2 Remains Precise Over Time

As a project moves forward, the value of a point must remain stable in order for the Dev Team to have precise points estimation. One way to do this is to use the same estimation process and logic throughout the whole project. Sadly, when a team is using a couple of reference Stories or if their definition of a point has been tainted by hours estimation, their estimation precision may drift over time. For example, if a Dev Team thinks of 1 point as having a value of 1 day of work, they will not estimate Stories using relative sizes, but will estimate in hours and translate this value in points. Over time, this team's skill will most likely improve and 1 day will deliver more work than what was possible at the beginning of the project. This creates a Drifting precision in their points estimation.

Imagine that this Dev Team has Story A in the original Backlog. Let's say this Story was evaluated at 5 points which for this Team really means 5 days. Later in the project the team is asked to estimate Story B which is exactly the same size as Story A. Because the team now has a better understanding of the project and its technologies, they estimate Story B at 1 point (1 day). The Backlog is now tainted by containing two Stories of exactly the same size but with two very different effort values (5 and 1). By creating a single estimation scale which remains unchanged for the duration of the project, CrumbScale prevents estimation drifting. Faced with the previous scenario, a team using CrumbScale would find where Story B fits in their Point Scale. Here the team is not thinking about time durations but is scanning the list for similar work (from a complexity-effort perspective). By finding similar work, like Story A which is part of the scale, the team will very likely give Story B the same effort value as Story A. The fact that the team skills are improving over time is now represented only through a change of sprint velocity.

Warning: Do not estimate completed work

It is important to mention why the zero was removed from the CrumbScale measure scale. The logic process used to estimate new work in effort points does not apply when looking at completed work. The cloud of uncertainty surrounding new work forces us to consider many scenarios and buffer our effort estimation accordingly. On the other hand, if we are asked to estimate work that we have already completed, our brain is tainted with the known outcome. A couple of strong decision-making biases[46] are working against us on this one. First is the *Curse of knowledge* making it hard to view other perspectives. Second is the *Well travelled road effect* where we grossly underestimate finished work and, compared to the known completed Stories, grossly overestimate the unknown of the new Stories.

8.3 Faster Estimation

Points estimation happens in two different ways during a project: the initial estimation of the Backlog, and the punctual estimation of new Stories during the Production Period. Surprisingly, while trying to avoid the need for reference Stories, the CrumbScale approach also proved to be faster at estimating the original Backlog and, even more surprisingly, ridiculously faster at estimating new stories.

---

[46] Wikipedia. *List of cognitive biases*. [Online] Available at: https://en.wikipedia.org/wiki/List_of_cognitive_biases [Accessed 4 Feb. 2017].

Initial Estimation

Using CrumbScale, we return to the two simple questions: "Is this Story bigger or smaller than that other Story?" and "Is this Story twice as big as that other Story?" For a majority of the Stories, the Dev Team will be able to answer those two questions without having to dive too deep into the details of the Stories. Instead of trying to single out an effort estimate for each Story one by one, the participants are sorting the whole list all at once. By sorting instead of estimating, the team is only looking for "Just enough" details to answer the two questions.

Using this method, teams were able to estimate 30 to 60 Stories per hour, depending on the team's experience and the project complexity. First time users must be able to estimate at least 20 stories per hour while CrumbScale experts will be able to estimate upwards of 90 stories per hour. CrumbScale was developed to support Backlogs of 400+ stories which were estimated in half a day using this method.

Saving even more time, this initial estimation of the Backlog will be the only points estimation event for the entire project. No re-estimation will ever be needed unless the project is changing so much that additional features are falling outside the team's expertise and can not be compared with the ones contained in their CrumbScale. I only had to do this once in a project where the entire technology stack was changed, mid project. This was in the context of a startup where the existing code base eventually became incompatible with the new target market.

New Stories

The initial time investment of estimating the entire Backlog really pays off later on in the project as the new Stories start pouring in. Using their CrumbScale estimation tool, the team can estimate a new Story in 30 seconds flat and have total confidence in the result.

Starting at the bottom of their CrumbScale, the estimators go up the list trying to find an item of similar type.

When the most similar item is found, they simply take its point value and assign it to the new Story.

8.4   Supports   More   Robust Predictability and Planning

By estimating all the known features, including all the *Must* features and their risks, you will create a point scale covering a substantial range of the project stories and thus have a reliable representation of the effort distribution. This effort distribution is essential to understand the relationship between the risks, the velocity and the project scope. Luckily this need for a meaningful amount of Stories is offset by the ability of CrumbScale to estimate large numbers of Stories in very little time.

A point scale which is a reliable representation of all the features is the main contributing factor to stabilizing the point estimations precision. With this stability, the team will be able to gain predictability over its effort velocity during their first 3 sprints (normally). In turn, stability and predictability will increase confidence while planning by projecting this velocity over the future sprints.

It's not all rosy. The one downside I have found while using this method is that a minimum number of stories is needed to produce a good CrumbScale. Minimally, a Backlog of 40 or more Stories is recommended. If you have less than that, you may have a harder time estimating new Stories or stabilizing your velocity. On the other hand, a 40 Story Backlog will be completed so fast that predictability will be mostly influenced by preparation, planning and expertise.

8.5 Complexity Distribution

Note: At the time this book was written, the following work was still theoretical but remained promising enough to share the concept.

This new idea touches back on the subject of precision. As explained before, traditional points estimation methods rely on the identification of reference Stories. Those first stories will most likely polarize the following estimations and, in turn, distort the distribution of points along the value of the scale. Trying to avoid this is almost a lost cause since our brain is, once again, working against us through more decision-making biases. The *Anchoring bias* is tricking us into clumping the new effort values close to the initial reference Stories. Another problem would be the *Framing effect* where the effort point value can end up being different when compared to a first reference Story or to a second one. As a workaround, the effect of both these biases could be reduced by having a reference Story for each value of the Point Scale, which means more estimations in hours and more unwanted parallels between hours and Points.

Even if the team manages to reduce or eliminate this bias effect, the simple act of selecting reference Stories may create a distortion in the data. Let's explain this through an example. The team decides to take two reference stories, one small with a value of 2 and one large with a value of 8. Using those two values has the double advantage of representing the high and low range of decent-sized points values while leaving space for smaller and larger Stories and, secondly, having a size ratio of ¼ between those two values will simplify the selection of those two reference Stories. So far so good, but in this very common scenario the team can make two mistakes: 1) One of the two stories must be "declared" as having a value of 2 or 8. This "educated guess" may be off the mark by 1, 2 or even 3 steps in the Points Scale and, assuming the team is right in their estimating the ratio (of ¼) between the two Stories, the resulting values for the two reference Stories could then be 1-4, 3-13 or even 5-20. This will shift the data left or right on the scale and, unless the team estimates a greater sample, they have no way to avoid this. 2) The estimated ratio between the two reference stories, which will most likely be estimated in hours, may not represent the ratio of the other stories estimated in points. In order to estimate in hours the team must dig deeper into their understanding of the reference Stories which reduces the unknown factor and, consequently, exposes the team to the kinds of problems plaguing the estimation of completed work (described before in this chapter). With this type of error, the ratio between the two Stories which may have been ⅛ if estimated in points could turn out be ¼ with a detailed hour estimation. Not getting the proper ratio between those reference Stories will introduce an error in the data.

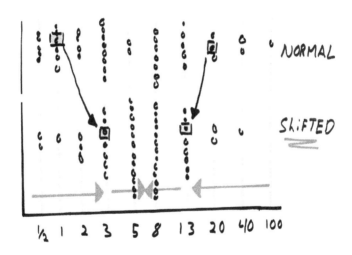

Figure 8.1 – Stretching and compressing data around the references

Luckily, with our current use of the traditional points estimation, this error in the point distribution along the point scale does not seem to have any impact. On the other hand, having an accurate representation of the point distribution may give us a new look into project where we may find patterns that could help us predict complexity, manage risk and gain predictability faster. We could view this point distribution as the fingerprint or the DNA of the project complexity. This raises more questions than answers, but this is the theory so far, and I hope something practical can emerge from the data.

A less serious final note...

I will end with this geek look at estimation, Vizzini style:

> "A clever man would estimate the stories in his Backlog, because he would know that only a great fool would jump blindly into a project. I'm not a great fool, so I can clearly not work without estimations. But you must have known I was not a great fool; you would have counted on it, so I can clearly not waist time estimating my entire Backlog instead of creating value.
>
> Because estimation comes from management, as everyone knows. And management is entirely peopled with criminals. And criminals are used to having people not trust them, as you are not trusted by me. So I can clearly not work without estimating thus reducing planning to guesswork.
>
> You must have suspected I would have known the estimation origin, so I can clearly not burden my team's morale by estimating stories.
>
> You've beaten my legacy system refactoring, which means you're exceptionally strong. So, you could have hidden unknowns in your feature demands. So I can clearly not choose to not estimate. But, you've also bested my biggest business problems which means you must have studied. And in studying, you must have learned that a developer is mortal so you would have removed the risks from your epics, so I can clearly not estimate this work."

PHILLIPE CANTIN

www.ingramcontent.com/pod-product-compliance
Lightning Source LLC
Chambersburg PA
CBHW052146070326
40689CB00050B/2318